MISSING PART OF THE SOUL

Swati Sarkar

Made with ❤ on the Notion Press Platform
www.notionpress.com

जिंदगी में ऐसे कुछ नज़्मे होते है, ऐसे बोहोत किरदार होते है, जो आखिर तक साथ नहीं चल पते है, पर उन टुकरो में भी छोटी छोटी जुन्दगी बास्ते है, कुछ लम्हे साथ देने वाले भी जिंदगी का हिस्सा होते है....

("In life, there are many poems, many characters, who cannot walk with us until the end, yet in those fragments, small lives also reside. Some moments, even those that stay with us briefly, become a part of our life. Even if the story remains incomplete, there is still meaning to be found in living through them...")

My wholehearted acknowledgement to Dr. Pratik P. SURANA (Ph.D) for trusting me with everything and giving me the rebirth as who I am today.

Thankful to my late father Sri Satya Mondal & my mother Smt. Radha Mondal & my uncle Mr. P.K. Sarkar for whatever they have done for me.

Let me feel high,
Let me fly…
Let me feel the sky,
Please don't cut my wings,
I want to fly…
Even high…
Don't stop me,
I may die,
My wings can't resist the rainfall,
So, I need to rest then,
But not my soul….
Let me fly, let me touch you.
Once more... in the sky.

As human beings, we are one of God's most beautiful and amazing creations. But the most special part of us is our soul. Our soul lets us feel deeply, connect with others, and experience life in ways that go beyond the physical. Though death comes to everyone, our souls live on—they are eternal. They just move from one body to another in the cycle of life and rebirth.

If I had a second life, I would want to come back as a butterfly. I've always been fascinated by their delicate wings—the reds, yellows, oranges, blacks, blues, and the beautiful patterns they carry. The colours and grace of butterflies attract everyone.

I dream of the day when I might become a butterfly—a symbol of change and beauty, flying freely in a world full of colour and wonder.

Contents

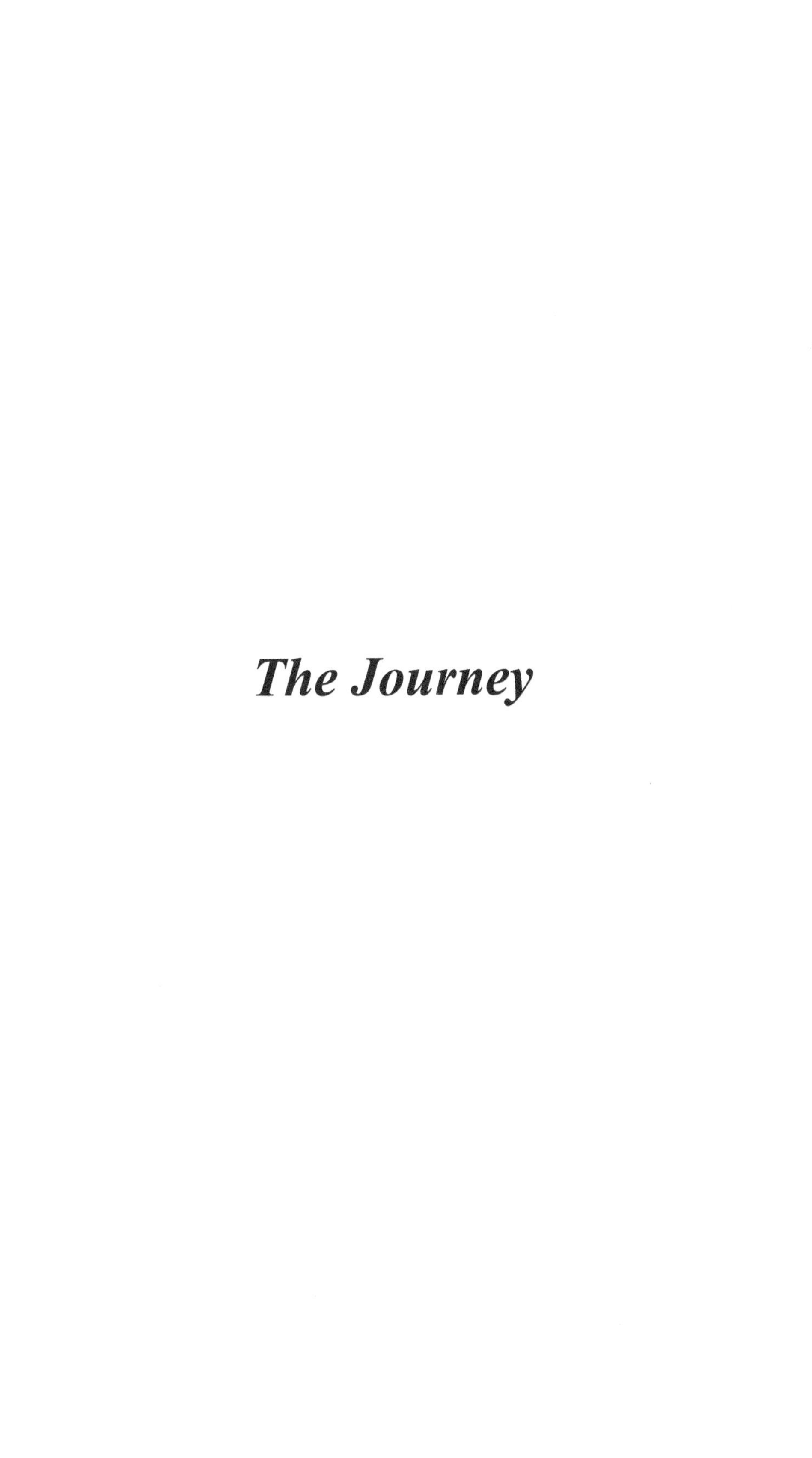

The Journey

Chapter I

Life is actually a journey—a journey of the soul. We travel from one point to another. According to philosophy, life is the combination of many journeys. We never know what is waiting for us at the next station.

"Time" is the most important aspect for all living beings. It's an asset for everyone.

Time means a revolution. Time is the most powerful gift.

I am talking about a time when there were no smartphones, no WhatsApp, no Facebook, no LinkedIn, not even Instagram. People used to write letters by hand.

Computers existed, but they were not as essential as today. Even cell phones were available, but only with minimal features. AI wasn't even a thought in human minds.

Most middle-class people travelled by train only. For the last 15 minutes, my train has been waiting at a station. I heard from my co-passengers that it's a big junction, so the train will be waiting here for some more minutes. My wristwatch says it's around 9:15 AM. I feel like I need to have my breakfast now.

This is the second time in my life that I am travelling alone. I feel a little awkward. There are so many people around me. It's a 3rd AC coach. I was travelling from Mumbai to Kolkata; it's a two-night journey. Back then, Mumbai wasn't even called Mumbai—it was Bombay.

The place was crowded and packed with people. I felt uneasy, especially since I couldn't see any women around me. I hadn't slept well the previous night – it was hard to rest in such a busy and uncomfortable environment.

Then I noticed the side lower berth was empty. The person who had been sitting there must have got off at this station. It looked cosier, so I decided to switch seats.

As soon as I made myself comfortable, he walked in.

He was tall and handsome, with an athletic build, curly black hair, and sharp, intelligent eyes that immediately drew attention. He was holding his ticket, checking the seat numbers, and then stopped right in front of me.

"Excuse me," he said, looking at me with a surprised expression. "I think this is my seat."

I felt a bit awkward but replied, "Oh, I'm sorry. If you don't mind, could you take my seat instead?"

He smiled and said, "No problem. Don't worry about it. You can stay here if you're comfortable."

Relieved, I said, "Thank you so much! My seat was a bit noisy, so I thought this one would be better. I hope I'm not bothering you."

He shook his head kindly. "Not at all. It's fine."

I felt a surge of confidence. After all, how could anyone refuse me? I may not look like Aishwarya Rai, but I know I have my own charm.

A little later, I decided it was time for breakfast. As a kind gesture, I offered him something to eat. He smiled and politely declined. "Thank you, but I already ate before boarding," he said.

There was something about him that made me want to talk. I'd been travelling alone since the evening before, starting from Bombay Central Station, and hadn't spoken to anyone yet. Normally, I'm shy and don't talk to strangers. But sitting there with him, it felt like a moment of change, as if I could take a chance and be someone new.

Still, a voice in my head reminded me that I was travelling alone, with no other women around, and I needed to be cautious. But despite that, I couldn't help feeling drawn to him.

His looks, his calm presence, and the way he carried himself – it all completely captivated me.

Chapter II

"May I know your name, please?" I asked, trying to keep my voice calm.

"Sure," he replied with a warm smile. "I'm Rishabh, Rishabh Malhotra. I'm a mechanical engineer, working with the Airport Authority of India as a ground engineer. And may I know about you?"

"I'm Sharmila, full name Sharmila Bose. I'm an artist," I said softly.

"Wow, nice to meet you, Sharmila. You must be Bengali—I can tell from your accent. If you don't mind me saying, you have a beautiful smile, and your teeth are perfect. Please keep smiling; you look amazing when you do," he said, his words confident yet kind.

I felt my cheeks flush. Compliments like that, especially from a stranger, weren't something I was used to. It made me shy and a little self-conscious.

Suddenly, I noticed the other passengers were watching us. Their curiosity was understandable—this was the first time I'd spoken to anyone on this journey, and being a woman travelling alone, I could sense their interest.

The train started moving again. It was still a long journey to Kolkata, with about 19 hours to go. Tea and coffee were being served, and the staff began taking lunch orders. I ordered two coffees and my meal. It was 10 a.m.

We sipped our coffee, and he asked, "So, do you work in Bombay, or were you visiting someone there?"

"No," I replied. "I was in Bombay to meet my childhood friend. I work in Kolkata."

"Nice! I live in Nagpur and am going to Kolkata on an official trip," he said. "I'll be staying at the Peerless Hotel for three days."

I kept my tone casual, not giving away much, even though his charm made it hard to stay indifferent. The less interest I showed, the more intrigued he seemed. It was like a little game—one I was enjoying more than I expected.

After finishing his coffee, he stepped out to the non-smoking zone. Without much thought, I found myself following him. Something about him pulled me in.

"Can I share your cigarette?" I asked, surprising even myself. It had been months since I'd done anything so carefree. But in that moment, I felt an overwhelming urge to let go of my stress. "No one knows me here," I thought. "Why not take this small risk?"

Who says only men can flirt? Women can too, as long as it's harmless and tasteful. I believed flirting was an art—when done well, it could be as light as a breeze.

"So," I said playfully, "how many girlfriends do you have?"

He caught on immediately, his eyes twinkling. "Does it really matter now? Let's forget about the past and the future. Let's just live in this moment," he said with a grin.

We returned to our seats, but I could tell he was eager to keep talking. I glanced at the time—only 11 a.m. We had hours ahead to share this little adventure.

Then, as if the universe were nudging me, I heard a quiet voice inside: *"Go, my child. Live your life for a few moments. After that, you will both go your separate ways."* ….. "जा बेटा, जी ले अपनी जिंदगी कुछ घोंटो के लिए, फिर वो आपने रस्ते, और तू भी आपने रस्ते"।

But I've always believed in honesty, no matter what. If this was going to be a meaningful connection, even for just a few hours, I had to tell him the truth—the hardest truth about me.

I wasn't sure how he would react, but I needed to see if he could handle it.

Chapter III

Another station arrived, and the train halted for a few minutes. New passengers boarded, while some got down. As the train started moving again, I smiled at Rishabh and pulled out a photo from my handbag. It was of a 3-year-old boy.

"Can you guess who this is?" I asked, showing him the picture.

He looked at it closely and said, "Wow, so cute! He must be a relative—let me guess... your sister's son? There's a resemblance."

I smiled again and replied, "No, he's my son."

Rishabh's eyes widened in surprise. "Your son? Are you serious?" He seemed genuinely shocked, as it was hard to believe. Back then, it was unusual for an Indian mother to be so slim, fit, and vibrant, especially one travelling alone.

"You must be joking! Or are you the Santoor soap mom from the ad?" he teased.

I laughed lightly, but before I could respond, he started asking the expected questions. "Where is he? Who's taking care of him? He must be with his father, right? Lucky man—your son is adorable.

But honestly, you don't look like a mother. You don't even look married!"

I kept smiling, choosing not to answer. I knew if I started explaining, the situation could spiral into something uncomfortable. But his curiosity wasn't going away.

He leaned in slightly, observing me. "If you're Bengali, married, and a mother, where are the signs of it? No *sindoor*, no bangles... Why are you lying?"

I replied calmly, "Does it really matter? Just a while ago, you told me to forget the past and live in the present. So, what's the issue?"

Rishabh looked serious now, his tone more concerned. "No, I need to know. Who are you? I assumed you were unmarried, like me."

I couldn't help but laugh at his earnestness. "What do you mean, Rishabh? Who am I? I've already told you! Fine, if you want the truth, here it is, I'm a single mother. I filed for divorce just a month ago. Now, does that answer all your questions?"

His face showed shock, but also respect. "I'm so sorry to hear that," he said after a pause. "But I can't believe it. How could anyone leave you? Is he blind?"

I replied, "It wasn't him who left – I left him."

Rishabh seemed taken aback by my strength. "That's brave. You're stronger than you look. It must have been a tough decision,"

I nodded, knowing he was right. Twenty years ago, society didn't accept divorced women, especially those with children, from middle-class families. The pressure was immense. The belief was clear and cruel: "इस घर से तुम्हारी डोली उठी है, अब अर्थी उठेगी तुम्हारी ससुराल से" ("Your bridal palanquin left from this house; now only your funeral bier will leave your in-laws' home.")

Women weren't allowed to raise their voices or leave, no matter how bad things were. But I had broken those rules.

"Don't be surprised," I told him with a small smile. "I know my worth, and I am capable."

He looked at me, impressed but cautious. "Let's not dwell on this. Forget who you are, who I am. Let's enjoy what we have today," he said.

I looked at him directly. "And what exactly do you mean by that?"

Without hesitation, he replied, "I want you to spend time with me. I'll be in Kolkata for three days. Let's meet there too. For now, we still have hours until tomorrow morning—let's make the most of it."

His boldness surprised me. "It's so easy for you to approach a single woman travelling alone, isn't it?" I said, my tone sharp. "Do you think I have no dignity or self-respect?"

He softened his tone but stood his ground. "You're misunderstanding me. I'm not saying anything wrong. I can't promise marriage or a future, but I'd like to be close to you, even if it's just for now. Please consider it."

I raised my voice slightly, unable to hold back anymore. "So, because I'm alone, you think I'm available? Who do you think you are? What do I even know about you?"

Our argument drew the attention of other passengers. Their eyes were on us again, but I didn't care. Some lines couldn't be crossed, no matter how charming the other person was.

Chapter IV

Time passed, and the tension between us eased into a comfortable silence. Rishabh, sensing the unspoken pain in my heart, tried his best to make me smile. He must have recognised that there was a fresh wound, one still bleeding beneath my brave exterior.

Life, I realised, has a way of testing us in the most unexpected moments. This was my test—a challenge to hold my ground and not let my emotions or vulnerabilities take over, even though my inner turmoil made it difficult to resist the fleeting comfort of companionship.

Lunch arrived, served by the train's catering staff. I took my plate, as I had already ordered, but noticed Rishabh hadn't brought anything to eat. He didn't even carry food with him. Without a second thought, I offered him some of mine. He accepted, albeit with a promise that he would arrange for his meal at the next station and share it with me.

True to his word, the train stopped at the next station within 20 minutes. One of Rishabh's relatives had come to deliver his lunch—a home-cooked meal prepared lovingly by his sister, who lived nearby. He returned to our compartment carrying a packet full of food and water.

As agreed, we shared his food, eating together from the same plate. The meal was simple but delicious, rich with the warmth of a sister's care. This was a first for me—sharing food so intimately with a stranger, someone I had known for only a few hours. Coupled with the earlier shared cigarette, it felt surreal, as though life had momentarily suspended its rules.

Yet, these small acts, this impromptu connection, created memories strong enough to last a lifetime. I couldn't deny the magnetic charm Rishabh exuded. It wasn't just his words or actions—it was the way he carried himself, the effortless way he made me feel seen and understood.

But I wasn't alone in noticing this connection. Our fellow passengers, about 6-8 of them, had been quietly observing us. I could feel their eyes, hear the unspoken curiosity in their expressions. My sixth sense confirmed it: "दो दिल मिल रहे हैं, मगर छुपके-छुपके... सबको दिख रहा है, मगर छुपके-छुपके... " ("Two hearts were meeting in secret... Everyone could see it, yet it was hidden in secrecy...")

The past year had been nothing short of transformative for me—a journey of loss, rediscovery, and resilience. My decision to separate from my husband with my 3-year-old son had turned my world upside down. People I once trusted, family and friends I held close, had become strangers overnight. Their judgement cut deep, their whispers louder than my cries for understanding.

In that moment, I realised how much I needed Rishabh. Not as a lover, not even as a friend, but as a reminder of something I had almost forgotten—how to live. Some people come into our lives for a fleeting moment, not to stay, but to teach us a lesson we carry forever.

That day, Rishabh gave me a kind of rebirth. His words, simple yet profound, have stayed with me all these years: *"Forget everything. Just live—live the moments you have today. Don't think beyond them. Who knows what tomorrow holds? When you achieve your goals, no one will know how hard the journey was for you or who stood by you through it. Be with yourself. Don't listen to others. This is your time to prove yourself. You are the creator of your own life. Celebrate each day as though it's your last."*

He was a stranger—someone whose path crossed mine by sheer coincidence, orchestrated by forces beyond my comprehension. Yet, he left an indelible mark on my soul.

Life, I realised, is never entirely in our control. What is meant to happen will unfold in its own time, its own way. That journey, that moment, and Rishabh's presence were not within my power to design, but they were exactly what I needed.

Chapter V

The sun is just about to set...

A beautiful sunset moment is like nature's grand finale, a symphony of colours that transforms the sky into a canvas of vibrant hues. The sun, low on the horizon, bathes everything in a soft, golden glow, casting long shadows that stretch lazily across the earth. As the sun slowly sinks, its light shifts from a warm amber to shades of pink, purple, and fiery orange, blending together in a mesmerising gradient.

The air becomes still, and time seems to slow down as the world is bathed in a peaceful calm. The clouds, if present, are illuminated from below, creating a stunning contrast against the deepening blues of the evening sky. The water, if nearby, mirrors the colours above, adding to the magic of the moment. Birds may fly across the horizon, silhouetted against the fading light, as day gently transitions into night.

In this fleeting moment, everything feels connected—the sky, the earth, and the quiet observer who stands in awe. There's a sense of peace, of completion, and perhaps a hint of nostalgia, knowing that this exact beauty will never repeat in quite the same way. It's a reminder of life's impermanence and the quiet beauty that exists in letting go of the day.

As we had our lunch a little late, around 5:30 PM, I started craving another cup of coffee. Rishabh didn't want any, as he's not fond of tea or coffee. But once I began sipping my cup, he asked me to share it with him. And again, I noticed everyone was staring at us. Rishabh started singing, "कुछ तो लोग कहेंगे, लोगों का काम है कहना..."—the great Kishore Kumar. I just smiled at him.

"Sharmila, do you know what the most beautiful part of you is?" Rishabh's voice was gentle, almost reverent, as he looked into my eyes. "It's your soul. You are so pure and gentle that people are easily drawn to you, but no one can truly touch you. You have a divine presence; you know how to protect yourself. You are the peace of the heart; you are the gentle breeze."

His words washed over me, leaving me simultaneously comforted and exposed. I hesitated for a moment before replying, my voice steady despite the storm inside me.

"Can you wait for me? I need more time," I said, each word weighed with sincerity. "I have so much to do. I need my divorce certificate first, and after that, I plan to relocate to another city for a career hike. If you can wait, let me know..."

He smiled—a smile that seemed to hold the wisdom of acceptance and the bittersweet pain of unspoken truths. "Who knows about tomorrow?" he said softly. "But I must say, you might not accept my proposal today. Still, once I get off this train, you'll go your way, and I'll go mine. However, I will remain in your heart forever. You will never forget me for the rest of your life, and that's my challenge."

His words struck a chord deep within me, igniting a flame I had tried so hard to keep extinguished. I wanted to respond, to tell him what I was truly feeling, but the walls I had built around my heart were too strong to let me speak. Instead, I murmured under my breath, almost too quietly for even myself to hear: "Who says I'm going to forget you? How could I forget you? I'm not trying to push you away—I'm just protecting myself from melting into you."

The train's rhythm was unchanging, a steady reminder of the journey that would soon come to an end. And yet, in that fleeting moment, it felt as though time itself had paused. The world around us faded, leaving only the two of us—two souls navigating the delicate balance between hope and reality, connection and restraint.

In the meantime, it had already gotten dark outside. All the lights came on automatically in the train. People were passing by here and there, as a 1-day and 2-night journey can be very boring — unless you have a charming, attractive, athletic, joyful person like me as a co-passenger.

Now it was literally tiring for me too—talking with a 'chatterbox' for so many hours, being observed by many people, and a sleepless night had all triggered my restlessness.

I stepped out of the compartment to get some fresh air, standing by the door and watching the world rush past. It was around 7:30 in the evening. The train felt quieter now, with people worn out from two long days of travel. As I stood there, lost in my thoughts, I didn't even realise when tears started rolling down my cheeks.

Barely 10-15 minutes had passed. My face was still turned toward the open door, the darkness outside reflecting the darkness in my mind. Suddenly, I saw Rishabh come out from the compartment, his eyes searching for something. There were other people standing nearby—some smoking, some talking. I didn't get a chance to wipe my tears before he saw me.

As I stood there at the door, lost in thought, he suddenly shouted, "Sharmila, what are you doing here? Why is the door open? I was looking for you." His voice pulled me out of my trance, and I turned to face him. That's when he noticed the tears on my face. Perhaps he thought I was about to do something drastic.

Without any warning, he came close, too close, and before I could react, he wrapped me in a tight hug. His arms were warm and firm, and I could feel his concern through the embrace. But what followed left me completely stunned. He pressed his lips against mine, gently but with an urgency that seemed to carry every unspoken word he wanted to say. He wiped my tears with his face, and then his lips claimed mine again, as if he wanted to replace the sadness with something else—something intense and unrestrained.

I lost track of time. The sound of clapping brought me back to reality. I pulled away, startled, realising that several passengers had witnessed the moment. They were clapping, cheering, and even whistling, as if we had just acted out the climax of a romantic movie. My face burned with embarrassment. I felt exposed, vulnerable, and deeply uncomfortable.

He held my hand tightly and led me back to our seats. I followed silently, unable to process the mix of emotions inside me. People were congratulating him as if he had just achieved something extraordinary. I couldn't bring myself to look up, not at him, not at anyone. I felt like disappearing, but there was no escape. The train kept moving forward, and we still had hours before reaching our destination.

Back at our seats, he tried talking to me, but I stayed quiet, refusing to meet his gaze. The embarrassment was too much. Dinner came and went; I had no appetite. Despite his insistence, I refused to eat, and in solidarity—or perhaps guilt—he didn't eat either.

He asked for my phone number again, like he had in the morning, but I didn't give it to him. I didn't even ask for his. I felt too overwhelmed, too drained.

Eventually, I decided to lie down, hoping that sleep would offer me some escape. He noticed my discomfort and quietly made my bed for me. Before I turned away, he said softly, "Wake me up in the morning when we arrive. Our destination is the same."

I didn't respond. I simply lay down and closed my eyes, though I knew sleep wouldn't come easily. The whispers and glances from the other passengers continued around us, a reminder of the spectacle that had unfolded. I felt trapped in that moving train, stuck between emotions I didn't want to face and a situation I couldn't escape.

Chapter VI

I woke up early and realised the train was about to reach Howrah station on time. There were another 15-20 minutes left. I rushed to freshen up as quickly as possible. I noticed Rishabh was still in deep sleep. I thought I wouldn't wake him up and would get down once the train reached the platform, as I didn't want him to know anything more about me. I didn't even feel the need to say goodbye.

I don't know exactly what happened to me.

The train reached the station, and everyone started getting off one by one. It was around 6 a.m. I also joined the line to get off. Suddenly, someone from the crowd called Rishabh, as the train was already at the platform. The more I avoided him, the more he persisted.

He woke up with red eyes, and again, our eyes met. He had been sleeping just above my seat on the upper berth. He got down from his berth and asked me why I didn't wake him up. I didn't say anything.

He again held my hand and asked me to wait for him. He ordered me to stay there and not go anywhere, as he would go with me.

I didn't want to create a scene like last night, so I just nodded and waited for him. He took another 5 minutes, grabbed my luggage along with his, and after we got down from the train, he took my left hand, wrote his phone number on my palm, and held my hand tightly. He insisted I call him, as he would be in the city for another three days. I was very sure I wasn't going to call him at all.

Meanwhile, we reached the taxi stand—the famous Yellow Taxi, only available in Kolkata.

No, thank you. No goodbye. Nothing.

I took my taxi to my destination, and he took his.

We separated, blending into the crowd in the City of Joy.

Once I got into the taxi, the very first thing I did was take out my cell phone and save his number. I knew I might not call him within those three days while he was in Kolkata, but I was sure I would call him once he went back.

He was right—I might not have talked to him in the last few hours, but he completely occupied my mind. I couldn't think about anything except him. I reached home and started working, but my mind was totally blocked. I was working like a machine, but my thoughts were consumed by his words. He had talked a lot. I found myself blushing, remembering those moments. I was getting mad, waiting to talk to him just once. I wanted to call him, just to hear his voice. I didn't want to say anything, I just wanted to listen to him. I started missing him so badly.

The incredible human mind, when deeply fascinated by someone, can become a powerful and consuming force. It's as though the mind enters a state of heightened awareness, where every action, word, or even a glance from that person feels magnified and deeply significant. This fascination ignites the brain's reward centres, releasing a flood of dopamine, which fuels intense feelings of excitement and longing. Time seems to warp—moments with them feel fleeting yet profound, while time apart stretches painfully.

In this state, the mind is constantly preoccupied with thoughts of the person, replaying memories, imagining future encounters, and crafting endless scenarios where deeper connections are formed. There's a pull towards them, almost like an invisible thread, making their presence not just wanted but needed. The person becomes the focal point, and everything else can blur into the background.

What's fascinating about this mental state is its ability to spark creativity, vulnerability, and introspection. The mind, in its obsession, can lead us to question our desires, fears, and boundaries, often pushing us toward growth. Yet, this fascination can also be overwhelming, where rationality is overshadowed by emotion, and we find ourselves yearning for an almost ethereal connection.

It's both a gift and a challenge, revealing the incredible depth of the human psyche and its capacity to be mesmerised by another being.

Chapter VII

As I was waiting to reach his home and completing the fourth evening, I called him from my cell phone number. I knew well that he didn't have my number. I called him for the first time, and my heartbeat was racing at 300 km/h. My hands were trembling unconsciously... I was just dying to hear his voice, even for once. The phone rang completely, but no one picked up. I was upset. My nature didn't allow me to make another call.

I just sat at my desk, upset, thinking about who would even remember a co-passenger from a train. It was just an infatuation. Suddenly, my phone started ringing... Oh my God! It was Rishabh.

I quickly answered, "Hello." He responded, "Why didn't you call me, Sharmila, for the last three days while I was in Kolkata? I was desperately waiting for your call. You didn't even give me your number, and I couldn't find you."

I was spellbound. I couldn't say anything, so I just asked, "How are you, Rishabh? How did you know this was my number?".

He said, "Ask yourself, Sharmila, how I know it's your number. I've been waiting for this call for the last four days, and now you're asking how I knew!" We spoke for another 4-5 minutes and then I ended the call. There wasn't really much to say from my side.

Being a person with a strong sense of self-respect, I couldn't bring myself to call him again, but my mind talked to him all day and night.

We used to send messages 2-3 times a week.

When we were travelling together, he told me his birthday was next month. I remembered that day and made a plan to call him to wish him on his birthday.

After a month, I called him on his birthday and received a very cold reception. I didn't feel the need to call him anymore.

I knew well that his life was different. He was very attractive, with a charming personality, a joyful nature, and a good career. There must be a long line of unmarried girls for him. I had nothing in comparison. I couldn't even offer anything from my side. I tried to focus on my career, as before.

Sometimes, I missed him a lot, going crazy just to hear his voice once. But as usual, I couldn't make calls from my cell phone, so I went to different STD booths to call him, just to hear the word "hello" from the other side. Human mind... just unbelievable.

One day, out of the blue, I received a beautiful *shayari* from his number. In the meantime, I discovered a new creativity had been born within me—I had started writing *shayaris*.

This was very unusual because my upbringing was solely in Bengali culture, and I wasn't even that good at Hindi. The only non-Bengali friend I had was Rishabh, with whom I barely spoke. But since I was always lost in thoughts of him, this ability to write Hindi poetry developed in me almost by default.

I had written over 100 *shayaris* missing him within just six months. Whenever I asked him to come to Kolkata, he would say, "I will come soon," and I would make myself happy just hearing that.

"आरज़ू है तुझे दूरसे देखनेकी,

तम्मना नहीं तुझे पानेकी,

मगर खोना भी नहीं चाती...."

("I desire to see you from afar, There's no longing to possess you, But I don't wish to lose you either...")

This little *shayari* he sent me that time.

"With my little knowledge of Hindi, I understood what he meant to say to me…"

"And I started trying to make my mind understand to just stay away…"

Just there was a small hope that maybe, someday, somehow, I might meet him again if it is destined by God.

After around six months, one day I received a call from a lady around 11 o'clock in the morning. She was crying on the phone and asking urgently, "I saw you saved his number in his phone. I need to know who you are." I was spellbound and asking myself, "Who am I?".

She said she is his legal wife… and that was enough for me to know. It felt like I had been creating a beautiful painting for the last 6 months, and someone came and splashed water on the whole painting, ruining it…

Chapter VIII

Sharmila Bose, 28, a single mother, artist, and graphic designer, has been navigating a challenging journey for the past year. She creates for local magazines and newspapers, using her art as a form of expression, but her real battle began a year ago—a battle for her existence, her identity.

This battle wasn't fought with brushes or sketches, but with the invisible forces of societal expectations, judgemental relatives, and distant friends. In the past year, Sharmila has realised that when you challenge the deeply rooted norms of society, you're often left standing alone. Support from those closest to her, the people she thought would stand by her, was absent. Yet, despite this, she continues to fight—not just for herself, but for the right to live life on her own terms, as an artist, a mother, and an individual unapologetically true to her own identity.

Her journey symbolises resilience against societal pressures, proving that true strength often comes from within, especially when the world around you remains indifferent.

In traditional Indian society, divorce has historically been stigmatised, particularly for women. A divorced woman was often viewed with suspicion, pity, or as someone who had failed to conform to societal expectations. Many saw her as a symbol of brokenness or blamed her for the end of the marriage, regardless of the circumstances.

Her choices were often scrutinised, and she faced double standards, with fewer freedoms compared to divorced men. In some cases, a divorced woman was seen as a threat, her independence misunderstood as rebellion. The expectation for women to prioritise family over personal happiness reinforced these attitudes, making it difficult for divorced women to find acceptance or support.

She is courageously standing against the deeply entrenched, gothic mindset of society that has long defined a divorced woman through a lens of shame and failure. In a world that often views her independence with suspicion, she defies the judgement and scrutiny cast upon her. She represents strength and resilience, challenging an outdated belief that a woman's worth is tied to the permanence of her marriage.

Sharmila knows deep down that she can't remain in Kolkata much longer. The city, once a canvas of her creativity, has now become a place of confinement—stifled not only by limited career opportunities but by the relentless monotony of isolation and the never-ending discussions surrounding her personal life. She yearns for change, a break from the suffocating judgements, and the silence that comes with it.

Her decision to leave isn't just about seeking professional growth; it's about reclaiming her spirit, her dignity.

Recently, she received her divorce decree, a final step in severing ties with a past that no longer serves her. She asked for nothing in return—not a single rupee in alimony or for the expenses of her 3-year-old child. To her, this battle was about much more than money. It was about her dignity, her self-respect, and the fierce independence she has always cherished.

Yet, as she prepares to move forward, unaware of what lies ahead, another battle is quietly brewing—one she hasn't anticipated. In a few days, her strength will be tested once again. But Sharmila, though scarred, stands ready. She knows the fight for her identity isn't over—it's just evolving.

The girl, Pallavi, keeps calling Sharmila 3-4 times a day, relentlessly questioning her about Rishabh. Though Sharmila met Rishabh once on a train, he remains nothing more than a stranger to her—no bond, no connection, no relationship. But Pallavi seems unwilling to accept that. She keeps pressing, asking how there could be so many interactions, so many text messages between Sharmila and Rishabh if they truly meant nothing to each other.

Sharmila feels trapped, unable to make Pallavi understand the reality of the situation. The messages had been casual, nothing more than exchanges between two people who happened to cross paths. Yet Pallavi's persistent questioning makes it feel like an interrogation, as if she's searching for a truth that simply doesn't exist. Despite her calm explanations, Pallavi's doubts linger, and Sharmila begins to feel the weight of being misunderstood, caught in a situation she never wanted to be part of.

Sharmila feels utterly helpless in a situation she never anticipated. The weight of it all is too much, and with no one to confide in, she realises how isolated she truly is. The matter is too delicate to discuss with friends or family, leaving her no choice but to handle it on her own. Reluctantly, she invites Pallavi to visit her, hoping that a face-to-face conversation might clear the confusion. Yet, even as she extends the invitation, she knows it's a risky decision, one that could either resolve everything or make things worse.

In the midst of this turmoil, Sharmila has tried repeatedly to contact Rishabh, the one person who could clarify things and ease the growing tension. But for days, his phone has been unreachable. She senses that Rishabh, too, is entangled in this mess, likely facing the same pressure from Pallavi. Yet, in this crucial moment, he is nowhere to be found, leaving Sharmila to fend for herself.

The irony is bitter—what started as a brief encounter during a 19-hour train journey has now spiralled into something far beyond her control. What seemed insignificant has become a source of immense distress, and she finds herself battling on two fronts: one, an external struggle with Pallavi's relentless questions, and the other, an internal fight against her own feelings of vulnerability and isolation.

Sharmila, though strong, is now caught between these battles, with no clear path forward, navigating each moment with caution and a sense of survival.

Pallavi agreed to meet Sharmila, but with an unexpected twist— since she was out of town, she mentioned that her brother would come to meet Sharmila in her place. Sharmila, though hesitant at first, considered that perhaps discussing the matter with a man might offer a more practical approach rather than an emotionally charged conversation. Maybe, she thought, this would be a way to clear the air and resolve things more logically.

With a heavy heart, Sharmila agreed. She wasn't eager for the upcoming meeting, but she felt cornered by the relentless pressure. The constant barrage of questions and the suffocating feeling of being trapped in a web of misunderstandings had become unbearable.

This, perhaps, was her chance to put it all behind her—to finally break free from the mess that had entangled her life for so long and reclaim her peace.

Yet, despite her decision, a quiet unease still lingered in her mind. Was this the right move? Would it bring her the closure she desperately sought, or would it only deepen the confusion? She hoped it wouldn't make things worse, but the weight on her shoulders had become too much to bear. At this point, she was willing to try anything, even if it meant stepping into the unknown, hoping for a way out of the darkness that had clouded her life for so long.

Chapter IX

Sharmila sat in the bustling coffee shop at Salt Lake City Centre Mall, observing the crowd around her. It was a new mall, barely a year old, and conveniently close to her rented apartment, where she lived with her young son and a house help. She had chosen this public place to meet Pallavi's cousin, Suraj, knowing that a crowded area would feel safer when meeting a stranger.

Suraj, an average-looking guy, greeted her with a polite smile, extending his hand for a handshake. Sharmila, uncomfortable with the idea of physical contact, especially with a man she didn't know, simply folded her hands and said, "*Namaste.*" She wanted to keep the interaction formal and respectful, sensing that the conversation ahead might not be easy.

Suraj began the conversation with an apology on behalf of Pallavi, explaining that his cousin was a 19-year-old teenager, still immature and deeply infatuated with Rishabh. Sharmila was surprised to learn that Pallavi hadn't even completed her studies and that she and Rishabh weren't married – they were living together, much to the disapproval of Pallavi's family.

As Suraj spoke, Sharmila started to see the bigger picture. Pallavi had met Rishabh in much the same way Sharmila had—during a train journey. She had moved in with him without her family's consent, completely swept up in her emotions. Pallavi's jealousy and insecurity had driven her obsession with finding out who this 'other woman' was.

Suraj revealed something that unsettled Sharmila further. He explained that when Sharmila and Rishabh got off the train together at Howrah station, someone from Pallavi's family had been there to pick up Rishabh. That person had seen Sharmila and Rishabh together, heading towards the taxi stand. This witness reported back to Pallavi, describing Sharmila as a "beautiful girl." Not knowing who Sharmila was, Pallavi had become consumed by jealousy, determined to find out everything about her. But what hurt Sharmila the most was learning that Rishabh had never mentioned her to Pallavi—not even to clarify the innocent nature of their encounter.

Suraj explained that Rishabh, being a good-looking guy, often attracted attention from women. He hinted that girls easily fell for Rishabh's charm, and Pallavi was no different. But he acknowledged that Sharmila's case was completely different—she had no romantic involvement with Rishabh and was now caught in the middle of this drama through no fault of her own.

Sharmila sat quietly, absorbing everything. She now understood that this was all a misunderstanding fuelled by Pallavi's insecurity and Rishabh's silence. But the realisation didn't lessen the burden of the situation. Sharmila found herself in a mess she had never anticipated, fighting to protect her dignity against unfounded suspicions. And while Suraj seemed reasonable, she knew the path ahead was still fraught with challenges.

In the midst of this conversation, Sharmila was battling two emotions—frustration at being dragged into a situation that wasn't hers to begin with, and sympathy for Pallavi, a young girl blindly in love, lost in her own insecurities. But what troubled Sharmila the most was Rishabh's complete absence in the matter—his silence and disappearance had left her to navigate this chaos on her own.

After finishing their coffee, Suraj began to shift the tone of the conversation. He tried to make Sharmila feel more comfortable, offering compliments that she hadn't asked for. His gestures became a bit more personal, and he praised her in ways that felt slightly out of place given the serious nature of their meeting.

Suraj mentioned that, while he had been told beforehand that the woman he was meeting was "beautiful,", seeing Sharmila in person had exceeded his expectations. "You're more than just beautiful," he said, his eyes lingering a bit too long. He went on to call her the perfect combination of "brain and beauty", praising not only her looks but also her intelligence.

Though his words were meant to flatter, Sharmila felt a sense of unease creeping in. What started as a polite apology for Pallavi's behaviour had now turned into something else entirely. She hadn't come here for compliments or to entertain any personal admiration from Suraj. Her focus was on clearing up the misunderstanding and moving on with her life.

Suraj's comments, though polite on the surface, left Sharmila feeling uncomfortable. She sensed a shift in the dynamic and realised that this meeting, which was supposed to resolve tensions, was taking an unwanted turn. Staying composed, she maintained a professional and distant tone, trying to steer the conversation back to the real issue at hand.

In her nervousness and rush to clear the air, Sharmila made an unexpected mistake. Feeling the pressure of the conversation, she blurted out something deeply personal: that she was a single mother, recently divorced, and struggling to establish her career. She also mentioned that she was planning to move to another city for a better opportunity. Her intention was to show Suraj that she had no interest in complicating anyone's life, least of all Rishabh's.

However, the moment those words left her mouth, Sharmila realised the gravity of what she had revealed. The conversation took a sharp turn, and she could sense the subtle shift in Suraj's demeanour. What had begun as a polite conversation quickly spiralled out of her control.

Suraj, taken aback, struggled to process this new information. He had sat across from Sharmila for the past half-hour, forming an impression of her as an intelligent, beautiful woman. But in an instant, learning that she was divorced and a single mother, something changed for him. In the eyes of society, a divorced woman carried a stigma, and for Suraj, who hadn't known anything about Sharmila's personal life before this meeting, the revelation was hard to digest.

The fact that Sharmila was not only beautiful and young but also educated, independent, and carrying the weight of societal judgement as a divorced woman made Suraj pause. Rishabh had never mentioned any of this to anyone, leaving Suraj to fill in the blanks with his own assumptions. In his mind, the image of Sharmila as a capable, self-reliant woman was at odds with the traditional expectations that often reduced a divorced woman to a social outcast.

Suddenly, the meeting became tense. Sharmila could feel Suraj's judgement lingering, not just about her relationship with Rishabh, but about her entire identity. For Suraj, this conversation was no longer about a misunderstanding between Pallavi and Rishabh; it was about reconciling his own preconceived notions about women like Sharmila—strong, independent, but unfortunately burdened by a societal label that he, too, found hard to shake.

Suraj seemed stuck in his own thoughts, grappling with the implications of Sharmila's revelations. His mind kept circling around a single question: "Are you a girl or a woman?" To him, the distinction felt monumental. The idea that someone he perceived as vibrant and full of potential could also be a divorced mother was difficult to reconcile.

He struggled to understand how it was possible for her to embody both identities—one that society often labelled as youthful and carefree, and another that came with the heavy burden of divorce and motherhood. Suraj's fixation on this dichotomy overshadowed the nuances of Sharmila's life, trapping him in a mindset that failed to appreciate her complexity.

As Sharmila returned home, she tried to shake off the awkwardness of her meeting with Suraj. She was still processing how a simple conversation had turned into an exploration of her identity and societal perceptions. Just as she thought she could finally relax, her phone rang—it was Pallavi again.

With a familiar tone of insistence, Pallavi asked the question that had now become a haunting refrain: "Are you a girl or a woman?"

Chapter – X

Sharmila sat in the dimly lit waiting area of the police station, her heart racing as anxiety and frustration gripped her. The minutes stretched into what felt like hours, each passing second amplifying the turmoil inside her. She was here to file an FIR, but against whom? The calls had become an unbearable nightmare over the past few days, each one worse than the last.

The voices on the other end were coarse and degrading, filled with insults and crude remarks. They suggested she was some sort of call girl, offering money, while others cruelly implied that, as a single mother, she was desperate for male attention to fulfil her desires. The humiliation of it all was suffocating, leaving her feeling exposed and stripped of her dignity.

"How can this be happening in my city?" Sharmila thought bitterly. The City of Joy, the place she had once called home, now felt like a foreign and hostile land. She had grown up believing in the safety and warmth of her surroundings, but now, those same streets seemed like a trap, imprisoning her in a society that refused to see her as more than her circumstances.

As a professional, she had always answered calls from unknown numbers, managing her work with grace and integrity. But now, that very professionalism felt like a liability, with her career caught in the crossfire of the disrespect she faced simply for being a single woman. Every call now felt like an assault on her identity.

Sharmila felt the weight of societal judgement bearing down on her, the relentless force of a world that sought to reduce women to their most vulnerable states. It felt as though her very existence was an offence, and she yearned for a sense of safety and respect that seemed increasingly out of reach.

After what felt like an eternity, a male officer finally approached her, his demeanour impassive and formal. He listened to her story with little more than detached curiosity. When she finished, he suggested, with casual indifference, that she change the SIM card linked to her number. Sharmila's frustration surged, a tide of anger rising in her chest. Was that really all she could do? She had come seeking justice, but all she was given was a suggestion that felt both dismissive and inadequate.

The officer's lack of empathy only deepened her sense of isolation. She had already changed her phone number three times in the past month, each time hoping for a respite that never came. The crushing realisation settled over her like a weight: this was her battle, and no one was going to fight it for her. She wasn't guilty of anything. She had done nothing wrong. Yet here she was, standing in a place meant for justice, forced to defend her dignity alone.

Her resolve began to solidify, growing stronger with each passing moment. She would fight this, even if it meant facing the battle by herself. She wasn't the problem here. And she wouldn't let anyone make her feel like she was.

With her back against the wall, Sharmila decided it was time to take control of her situation. She would fight this battle on her own terms, armed with the understanding that she had the strength and resilience to navigate the challenges ahead. She would not allow anyone—whether it was faceless callers or a dismissive officer—to dictate her worth or her path.

Embracing her determination, Sharmila resolved to reclaim her narrative, step by step. She would confront the harassment, seek the respect she deserved, and ultimately carve out a space where she could thrive as both a woman and a mother. This was her life, and she would fight for it, no matter the obstacles in her way.

The situation had transformed Sharmila in ways she never expected. The girl who once struggled to speak up, whose voice barely rose above a whisper, had found her strength in the face of adversity. No longer the shy, timid woman who felt cornered by judgement and harassment, she had become a powerful advocate for her own dignity.

With every challenge she faced, Sharmila discovered a newfound resolve. Each degrading call and dismissive comment from others fuelled her determination to fight back. She began to raise her voice,

Embracing her inner warrior, Sharmila started to speak out against the injustices she faced. Whether it was confronting the callers with unwavering confidence or sharing her story with others who might listen, she reclaimed her narrative. She understood that her fight was not just personal; it was a stand against a system that sought to diminish women like her.

In this transformation, Sharmila became a symbol of resilience. She learned to harness her voice, using it as a tool to challenge societal norms and assert her identity. No longer afraid of judgement, she stood tall, ready to confront anyone who tried to undermine her worth. This was her journey, and she would navigate it with courage and conviction, proving that even in the darkest moments, one could rise and shine brightly.

Determined to take control of her situation, Sharmila began answering the calls with a newfound strategy. She muted the voices, focusing instead on collecting the phone numbers. Within just a few days, she identified that most of the disturbing calls were coming from only 2 to 5 numbers, including two landlines.

Fortuitously, she remembered a colleague whose girlfriend worked at the telephone exchange and another contact in a mobile company. With their help, she managed to gather information about the numbers. It turned out they were all registered with a single mobile provider, the only one operating in the area at that time.

In a matter of days, she had not only uncovered the names and addresses associated with the numbers but also pinpointed their location: Khidirpur dock, a known hub of antisocial activity in Kolkata. The realisation sent a chill down her spine. She understood all too well that this area was fraught with danger, especially for a woman alone. It was also a predominantly Muslim neighbourhood, adding another layer of complexity to her already precarious situation.

Sharmila felt a mix of fear and resolve. While she had the information she needed to confront the source of her harassment, the prospect of going to such a dangerous area alone was daunting. However, she also understood that this was a crucial step in her fight for justice and dignity.

She began to consider her options: could she enlist the help of friends or family for support? Or perhaps there were local organisations that could assist her in addressing the situation safely? The thought of facing this head-on without help was overwhelming, but Sharmila knew she couldn't allow fear to dictate her actions. This was her battle, and she was determined to see it through, no matter the risks involved.

"Where there is a will, there is a way."

Suddenly, Sharmila received a call from a contact within the Kolkata police, a plainclothes officer who was willing to assist her if necessary. Encouraged by this newfound support, she had an intuition to reach out to Suraj again. Since she had changed her number, he wouldn't recognise it.

When she called, Sharmila spoke straightforwardly, determined to uncover more about the situation. To her surprise, Suraj revealed that Pallavi was not who she claimed to be. In fact, Pallavi was a fake name; the girl was actually Muslim and had 4-5 brothers involved in the harassment. Their intention was clear: to create chaos in Sharmila's life and keep her away from Rishabh.

Sharmila couldn't help but laugh at the absurdity of it all. The lengths to which they had gone to intimidate her were both ridiculous and infuriating. Suraj, it turned out, was just a neighbour of this girl, unwittingly caught in the web of drama that had unfolded.

With this new information, Sharmila felt a surge of empowerment. Knowing the truth behind Pallavi's facade and the motives of her brothers only fuelled her resolve to confront the situation head-on. She realised that the threats and harassment were not just random acts; they were a calculated effort to undermine her.

Armed with this knowledge and the support of the police, Sharmila was ready to take her next steps. The laughter that bubbled up in her was a reminder that she wouldn't be intimidated by their attempts to control her life. Instead, she would use this knowledge as a weapon in her fight for dignity and respect.

Chapter XI

While the police jeep (back then, the police only used jeeps) sped toward the location, Sharmila's mind was flooded with a whirlwind of thoughts. She was a simple, ordinary girl, married at the age of 22 after completing her studies in a respected family. Her in-laws showered her with love and respect, and she had never ventured out alone. But today, she found herself in an entirely different world, staying alone with her three-year-old son and now embarking on an unexpected mission. She was under immense pressure, seeking justice for herself, heading to a place where neither her family nor her friends would ever dare to go.

During these days, she had been learning computer courses, determined to upgrade her skills and design abilities. Soon, she would be moving to another city in India, already receiving interview calls for new opportunities. Yet, before leaving Kolkata, there was one thing she needed to finish. Once called the "City of Joy," Kolkata had now become a place of deep pain for her.

As computers began to grow more familiar and in demand, Sharmila started embracing the digital world. She had learned how to navigate the internet, discovering not just its vast resources but also the emerging realm of social networking. With old friends gradually distancing themselves from her, she found solace in new connections online. Two popular platforms of the time, "Match. com" and "Orkut," were gaining popularity, offering her a fresh circle of acquaintances and a new sense of belonging.

The world was becoming more connected, bringing everyone closer than ever before.

They finally arrived, but it took another ten minutes to locate the actual address, as the GPS system hadn't yet been introduced.

Without wasting a moment, Sharmila and her friend hurried up the stairs, knowing the office was located there. It was tucked away in a narrow alley, a typical galli.

When they reached the office, they found the room empty. The ceiling fan was still whirring lazily above them, but no one was in sight. The time was around 4:30 PM, with the sun still lingering in the sky. Sharmila and her friend decided to wait, as the office boy had informed them that Babu—the term used for the boss in Kolkata by the office servant—was there just moments ago. He had no idea where Babu had suddenly disappeared to.

Sharmila and his friend understand when they are asking for the address meanwhile "The Babu" got the news of coming a police jeep who looking for him, so he run away somewhere nearby. So, there is no point of waiting more. Sharmila just put her visiting card on the table, and she has enough confidence that the visiting card will do its job well.

Sharmila's intuition had been spot on. She reached home within an hour, just as the landline began to ring. It was 6 o'clock, and her son was out for his tuition class, accompanied by the house assistant. She calmly picked up the receiver, only to hear an enraged voice shouting from the other side:

"How dare you come to my office with the police? Who the hell do you think you are?"

Sharmila didn't flinch. Instead, she smiled, her voice steady as she replied to the unseen man on the other end.

"Haven't you figured it out yet? Listen carefully. I am *Maa Durga*. I am a woman, a mother, and I have invisible ten hands. I can do anything and everything to protect myself, my family, and my dignity. If I get even one more call from you or any of your numbers, I won't be visiting your office next time. I'll come to your home. Consider yourself warned."

With those words, she hung up, her resolve unshaken.

Chapter XII

Sharmila had relocated from Kolkata six years ago. Now settled in a new city, surrounded by new people, life had become more stable and peaceful. The world around her had also transformed dramatically, especially in the digital realm. 'Orkut' had vanished, replaced by the ever-expanding "Facebook," which brought with it a new wave of connection—people reconnecting with old friends, finding community in this vast virtual landscape. It was more than just social networking; it was a revolution, especially in India, where the IT sector had boomed at an incredible pace, reshaping careers, opportunities, and lives. The world felt smaller, yet more connected than ever before.

One sudden day, when Sharmila was working at her office and checking her friend's messages on Facebook, she was suddenly surprised to see a new friend request in her Facebook account.

Rishabh Malhotra! My goodness. She is surprised. Same face, suddenly all those incidents go through her mind. That great Mr. Rishabh! Missing person for so many years!

Sharmila feels to check with that. She accepted his friend request. And is waiting for his response.

2 days gone, no response. Suddenly, one afternoon after lunch hour, she started receiving messages from Rishabh Malhotra.

Hi Sharmila,

How are you?

I was finding you for a long time

My old number was not yet with me.

So, I lost your contact number too.

I want to meet with you.

It's very urgent.

Please allow me to meet you.

I want to apologise for what has happened between us, even though I only had a rough idea.

Where are you located these days?

I want to come.

Where are you?

Kolkata?

Delhi?

Mumbai?

Pune?

Hyderabad?

Please tell me where you are?

I was utterly spellbound, unsure of what to even write. Finally, I typed, *"Do you have any idea what your girlfriend did to me? How could I possibly allow you to meet me again? Am I a fool? I don't want to go through hell again."*

He replied, *"Please, listen to me. Give me a chance to explain, to be heard."*

After a few days of back and forth, we set a date for him to come to my city and meet me.

The human brain and its emotions—no one can truly resist them or fully understand their complexity. Here I was, allowing the same man I once craved so desperately, the same man who had dragged me into a hellish situation, to re-enter my life. Imagine that!

The day finally arrived. I invited him over to my home after work, as it was a weekday. When he entered the room, I immediately noticed a subtle change in him. Perhaps age and experience had given him a certain maturity that wasn't there before.

After offering him some snacks and coffee, we sat down, face-to-face. I could sense that he was preparing to say something important, though for a while, we kept the conversation light, discussing general topics. He seemed calm now, no longer the same restless person I had met during that 19-hour train journey so long ago.

Then, with a deep breath, he began telling me his story. He confessed everything. He apologised sincerely for the pain I had endured because of him, admitting that he had been trapped in a situation beyond his control. He explained how not everyone had liked the "decent Sharmila Bose." It was as if he had been caught between two worlds, and in the process, I had been hurt.

In that moment, I realised how much had changed—not just for him, but for me as well.

He explained that he had met the girl during a train journey, and, like many, he had started flirting with her. She was travelling with her brother, and they were from Kolkata. Over time, she became infatuated with Rishabh. However, he later discovered that she belonged to the Muslim community and was entangled in some dubious business affairs.

Feeling scared due to his government job, Rishabh tried to distance himself from her. But then the girl moved from Kolkata to Nagpur, determined to marry him, which made Rishabh even more apprehensive. Her constant accusations and nagging only added to his stress.

Things took a darker turn when she filed an FIR against him in Nagpur for physical assault and rape. Rishabh was arrested, and the girl's family pressured him to marry her to secure his release. Faced with the risk to his job, Rishabh and his family reluctantly agreed.

For four long years, he endured a relationship that became a living nightmare. The girl's obsession turned her behaviour erratic, and everyone around them grew increasingly irritated. She was essentially a mental health crisis waiting to happen. Eventually, she realised she couldn't control Rishabh, and after a year-long divorce process due to their different communities, she left for Dubai to stay with her cousins.

As he spoke, I listened intently, trying to discern whether he was telling the truth. I began to share my own story, explaining how she had hurt both of us. Rishabh admitted that she was capable of anything, and his eyes reflected the weight of regret he carried.

In the end, he expressed a need for my forgiveness, believing it would help him heal from the regrets of his past. He mentioned that his sisters were now looking for a "normal" girl for him to marry, and he felt it was essential to seek my apology before moving forward with his life.

Somehow, I felt this encounter was a necessary lesson for his past flirtations and overconfidence. I couldn't help but laugh and told him that perhaps he had learned from his mistakes and should approach his future with a gentler demeanour. He nodded in agreement, acknowledging the truth in my words.

After I had arranged dinner, I invited him to eat, and he accepted graciously. I assumed he would leave after the meal, especially since I lived alone in my apartment. However, after dinner, he surprised me by saying he wanted to stay the night and would leave early in the morning, mindful of my office schedule.

I was taken aback but remained composed. I could sense the tension in the air, the unspoken emotions swirling between us. As I prepared for bed, I wondered what this night would hold for both of us.

Life is a perfect circle, and you can't deny its patterns. Six years and six months ago, I had been waiting for this very day. I had poured my heart into my feelings, believing that if I waited sincerely, he would eventually come to meet me. My trust in that hope never wavered.

Now, as he sat in my living room, I reflected on how time had brought us back together, weaving our paths once more. It felt surreal, yet somehow destined, as if all the struggles and heartaches had led us to this moment. I realised that my faith in our connection had not been in vain; perhaps this was the closure—or the new beginning—I had longed for.

He whispered in my ear, *"Something that began six years and six months ago is meant to come full circle today."*. As he spoke, I felt the walls I had built around my heart begin to crumble. Two hearts, once apart, were now starting to melt together again. In that moment, I realised I had no reason to hold back any longer. I allowed myself to lean into him, to melt in his arms, feeling the warmth and connection, we once shared. It was as if time had stood still, and everything else faded away.

The End

The Devil's Tree

Chapter I

The **Devil's Tree**, known by many names across regions, is called **"*Saptaparni*"** in West Bengal, where seven leaves form a graceful cluster. But the true magic of this tree lies not only in its leaves but also in its flowers. Twice a year, in March and October, its blooms appear, marking the change of seasons. The fragrance of the flowers is mesmerising—so potent and alluring that it captivates the senses, leaving spellbound, almost as though one has been intoxicated by its delicate perfume.

The *Saptaparni*, or Devil's Tree, holds a mysterious and captivating presence in nature. As evening approaches, this tall, elegant tree releases a delicate, sweet fragrance from its clusters of small, cream-coloured flowers, filling the air with an enchanting perfume. It's a scent so distinctive that it draws you in, subtle yet profound, like a quiet whisper from nature itself.

This tree, often considered sacred and deeply connected to local folklore, blooms in the late autumn when most other flowers have faded. Its fragrance fills the night air with an almost magical aura, lingering like a gentle reminder of nature's hidden beauty and power. Walking near a blooming *Saptaparni* in the evening feels like stepping into another world where the perfume connects you to something timeless and sacred, evoking a sense of peace and quiet wonder.

The *Saptaparni* is more than just a tree; it's an experience, a fleeting yet profound reminder of nature's grace, which continues to surprise and captivate all who cross its path. Its flowers speak in silence, inviting us to pause, breathe deeply, and remember the quiet, magical moments that nature gifts us.

Ruchika eagerly looks forward to these seasons, enchanted by the intoxicating aroma of the Devil's Tree. It's as if she's addicted to the rich fragrance, which is strongest in the calm of the morning or the stillness of the evening. In these moments, nature seems to embrace her in a symphony of colours and scents, a beautiful reminder of her timeless beauty.

Today, the **7th of March**, is an especially important day for Ruchika. She turned 23 just three months ago, and having recently completed her graduation, she has now been accepted into a master's degree programme in geography. Ruchika has always been a dedicated student, and her beauty is matched by her intelligence. She's quiet, calm, and not very talkative, so her circle of friends is small, but her warm and gentle nature has made her beloved by her family. She also has a younger brother who's still in school.

Two months ago, Ruchika attended a friend's wedding, where someone noticed her. Later, they reached out through a friend and visited her home with a marriage proposal. While Ruchika's mother wasn't ready for her daughter to get married just yet—she wanted Ruchika to complete her studies, secure a good job, and only then think about marriage—Ruchika's father saw the proposal in a different light. The family that had proposed was respectable, and the groom, **Amit**, was handsome with a charming personality. However, one concern bothered him: Amit came from a business family, while Ruchika had been raised in a household of government employees. Ruchika's father worried that this difference in background might create challenges for her in the future.

But as the saying goes, "Pairs are made in heaven." Amit's family was determined to secure the match, and eventually, they arranged a meeting between Ruchika and Amit. Both liked each other, but Ruchika's mother insisted they wait until she finished her master's degree and secured a job.

Unfortunately, Amit's family was not willing to wait any longer, as Amit was already 29. They began pushing for an early marriage. This left Ruchika's father feeling conflicted—he wasn't financially ready for a wedding yet. Their focus had been on Ruchika's education, and her younger brother was still in 12th grade. The timing didn't feel right to him.

Amit, however, understood their concerns and reassured the family. He emphasised that they wanted a simple wedding and didn't expect any extravagant expenses or dowry. Amit's family was willing to take care of anything extra if needed. This eased Ruchika's father's worries, and he eventually agreed to the marriage. Despite the financial constraints, they began preparing for the ceremony, determined to make it special since it was the first wedding in their family. Although the budget was modest, the love and care they put into the preparations made it a meaningful event for everyone involved.

Ruchika felt a sense of joy today that was new, a gentle warmth growing in her heart. She had started to develop feelings for Amit, her soon-to-be husband. Although for her, this marriage had been arranged, she now understood that for Amit, it was more than that. He had confessed that the moment he saw her at his cousin's wedding, it was love at first sight. In a way, their union was a blend of both love and arrangement—half love, half arranged.

Their wedding was set for March, and today, Ruchika woke up early for some traditional rituals. After the morning preparations, she slipped away to the terrace of her family's home, drawn by the calming scent of the **Devil's Tree** just outside their gate. Its flowers were in full bloom, filling the cool morning air with their rich, mesmerising fragrance.

Her house was alive with relatives—most of whom were still asleep—while her mother, four aunts, her brother, and a few cousins had woken early for the ladies-only ritual. But once the rituals were done, Ruchika quietly sought solitude on the terrace, away from the noise and chaos. Standing under the vast sky, she took a deep breath, letting the sweet scent of the **Devil's Tree** surround her.

Suddenly, a wave of emotion swept over her, and she felt tears welling up in her eyes. She was about to leave this home, the place where she had spent her entire life, and move into a new one, a world that would be unfamiliar. Even the comforting fragrance of this tree, which had been a constant presence in her life since childhood, would no longer be with her. She thought back to when she was 12 years old, during a visit to Shantiniketan, where she had first fallen in love with this scent. She had asked her father to bring home a small sapling of the tree. Now, that little plant had grown into a full tree, and its blooms had become part of her everyday life.

She smiled, remembering the great **Rabindranath Tagore**, who wrote many of his timeless works under the shade of the **Chatim Tree**—the same *Saptaparni* tree in Shantiniketan. Its whispers had inspired him, and in that moment, Ruchika felt the same quiet inspiration.

The thought of not having this tree at her new home felt like a small loss, but then she smiled again. She would ask Amit to plant a Devil's Tree in their new house, and that idea comforted her. It made her feel that a small piece of her old life would still be with her in her new one. As she stood there, her mother's voice broke her thoughts: "Ruchika, where are you?" With a deep breath, she wiped her eyes and went downstairs.

The day moved forward, and the marriage rituals began. Ruchika was fasting today, a traditional part of a Bengali wedding where both the bride and groom don't eat until the ceremony is over. Fasting wasn't something Ruchika was used to, and as the hours passed, she began to feel the hunger setting in.

Her mind wandered to the future. Ruchika didn't know much about household work, as her mother had always encouraged her to focus on her studies. She wanted Ruchika to build a career first, believing that everything else—marriage, home life, and responsibilities—would come with time. But life had taken an unexpected turn with this sudden marriage proposal. Yet, standing there in the midst of all the wedding preparations, Ruchika felt hopeful. Though there were uncertainties, the love she was beginning to feel for Amit brought a sense of calm, and the idea of their future together—along with the comforting fragrance of the **Devil's Tree**—made her heart a little lighter.

As Ruchika prepared for this new chapter in her life, she learned more about Amit's background. His mother had passed away when he was very young, leaving him with the responsibility of caring for his younger brother. This knowledge deepened Ruchika's sense of responsibility for the new family she was about to join. A swirl of emotions—anticipation, nervousness, and hope—flooded her as she stepped closer to her future.

The wedding was set for around 9 p.m., and right on time, the makeup artist arrived. Once her bridal makeup was complete, Ruchika looked breathtaking, a vision in her wedding attire. As she sat waiting, her father entered the room to check on her. In that quiet moment, Ruchika noticed tears welling up in his eyes. It was a poignant reminder of how difficult it is for a father to give away his daughter. The bittersweet emotions filled the room—his love, pride, and the ache of letting go of someone so dear.

Ruchika took a deep breath, trying to steady herself, and once again, the familiar aroma of the **Devil's Tree** flowers filled the air. Sitting by the window, with the tree just outside, she let the soothing scent wash over her. The fragrance was a comforting reminder of home, wrapping around her like a gentle embrace. In that brief moment, Ruchika found a sense of peace amidst the whirlwind of emotions surrounding her wedding day. The blossoms' scent, deeply tied to her memories, calmed her nerves, reminding her that while she was about to leave one home, she would be building another, filled with new moments and experiences.

Chapter II

It was around 7 o'clock in the evening, and Ruchika sat on an elegant couch, glancing around as guests began to arrive for her wedding. Relatives were bustling about, attending to everyone's needs, but Ruchika's mind was elsewhere. A flicker of worry crossed her face as she wondered why her friends hadn't shown up yet. Just then, she spotted Ananya, her childhood friend, walking toward her with a warm smile. Relief washed over Ruchika, and she returned the smile. Her father had rented a banquet hall for the wedding, a bit far from home, but she knew it would take time for everyone to arrive. Soon, other familiar faces appeared, and her heart felt lighter.

As guests greeted Ruchika, showering her with compliments about her beautiful makeup and the upcoming wedding, she smiled, though her heart raced with anticipation. Suddenly, one of her cousin brothers shouted excitedly, "The groom has arrived! The groom has arrived!" His voice echoed through the room, stirring a wave of excitement among the guests. People began moving toward the entrance to catch a glimpse of her soon-to-be husband.

Ruchika's mother and aunts quickly sprang into action, gathering everything needed for the rituals to welcome the groom and his family. The air buzzed with joy and anticipation as the ceremony began to unfold.

However, Ruchika found herself sitting alone in the marriage hall as her friends rushed off to see Amit. The bustling excitement around her only heightened her nerves. Thoughts spiralled in her mind—worries about the new family she would be joining, the overwhelming process of a traditional wedding, and the uncertainty of life after marriage. She had heard so many stories filled with rumours about what happens after the wedding, and a quiet fear settled within her.

Taking a deep breath, Ruchika tried to calm herself, reminding herself that everything would be okay. Just then, her friends returned, buzzing with excitement. They couldn't stop talking about how handsome Amit looked, playfully teasing her. Ruchika felt herself blush, shyly smiling as they eagerly described him. For a moment, their joy washed away her nervousness, and a soft smile graced her lips.

Within half an hour, Ruchika's brothers and brothers-in-law arrived to escort her to the marriage venue. The excitement was palpable, but a small hiccup arose—both families realised they had forgotten to inform the marriage registrar in time, missing the one-month notice required for official registration. After a brief discussion, they decided to proceed with the wedding ceremony as planned and handle the legal registration afterward.

Though the situation could have caused tension, the families quickly found a solution, and everyone's focus shifted back to the celebration ahead. Now surrounded by her loved ones, Ruchika felt a bit more at ease, knowing that the most important part of her journey was about to begin.

Ruchika's nerves were at an all-time high as she sat on the small, flat wooden platform known as a *"piri,"*, her heart racing.

Her brothers lifted the *piri,* carrying her around Amit, who stood surrounded by the crowd's enthusiastic cheers. The sound of the pandit ji chanting loudly filled the air, heightening the intensity of the moment.

With her face covered by "pan leaves," Ruchika couldn't see anything. All she felt was the rush of movement beneath her, and with each turn, her fear of falling grew. She clutched the sides of the *piri* tightly, screaming inside, terrified she might topple over at any moment. The excitement of the ritual was overwhelming, but she held on, hoping for a smooth passage through this chaotic moment.

Then came the moment of "happy vision," the first time Ruchika and Amit were to look at each other during the marriage ceremony. As she lifted her face slightly, the guests erupted in cheers, encouraging the couple to meet each other's gaze. Ruchika's heart raced, and her cheeks flushed a deep shade of red from shyness. She couldn't bring herself to look directly at Amit; her eyes nervously darted away, despite her friends playfully urging her to focus on him.

She could sense Amit smiling warmly at her, which only deepened her embarrassment. The joy and excitement surrounding them felt overwhelming as she battled the swirl of emotions inside her. Pandit *ji's* voice broke through the noise, announcing the start of the "*Varmala*" ritual, where the bride and groom exchange garlands. This beloved tradition was met with cheers from the guests, but all Ruchika could think about was the fear of falling off the "*piri*" while trying to place the garland around Amit's neck. She took a deep breath, trying to steady herself as the ritual unfolded, trusting that her brothers would hold her securely.

Once all the rituals were complete, Ruchika and Amit were brought to the centre of the hall, where pandit ji sat, preparing for the next part of the ceremony. The sacred fire flickered warmly beside them as he began chanting again. It was already 9 o'clock, and the ceremony was set to continue for another three and a half hours. Ruchika started to feel tired, her body heavy with sleep and hunger, but she knew the most important moment was yet to come.

Finally, the time arrived for Amit to apply *sindoor* (vermilion) to Ruchika's hairline—a beautiful, unforgettable moment in every girl's life. As he gently applied the *sindoor*, a quiet hush fell over the room. With that simple act, Ruchika was officially declared married in the eyes of society.

She looked stunning, her face glowing as the *sindoor* graced her forehead, but her eyes began to well up with tears—partly from the intense emotions of the day and partly from the heat of the sacred fire burning nearby. The flames filled the atmosphere with warmth, mirroring the emotions swelling within her heart, which felt the weight of a new chapter in her life.

Chapter III

Ruchika found herself in a room filled with close relatives, her two best friends, and her new husband, Amit. In many Indian weddings, there's a funny tradition where everyone gathers around the newlyweds, playfully teasing them with jokes and light-hearted chatter. This moment was meant to break the ice and ease any awkwardness, making their introduction more comfortable.

Though Ruchika was tired from the day's events, she couldn't help but smile at the jokes being thrown around. Her friends joined in, their laughter creating a warm and familiar atmosphere. The teasing was harmless, filled with the kind of humour that made her cheeks flush once again. This shared moment with family and friends was a special part of the wedding night—a blend of light-hearted embarrassment and affection, crafting memories that would be cherished for years to come.

At some point, Ruchika drifted off to sleep, lulled by the comforting presence of her loved ones. She awoke suddenly to find that everyone around her had fallen asleep, exhausted from the festivities of the previous day. Feeling the need to freshen up, she quietly got out of bed. Just as she stood, Amit gently caught her hand, pulling her towards him.

Caught off guard, Ruchika lost her balance and tumbled into Amit's arms. He lifted her chin, brushing her cheek with his fingers before placing a soft kiss on her closed eyes. In that moment, the world around them faded away. Still wearing her beautiful red Banarasi saree, Ruchika felt a wave of shyness wash over her. The sudden intimacy left her heart racing, and she glanced around nervously, worried that someone might see them. The thought of being caught in such a tender moment made her cheeks flush with embarrassment.

Quickly managing to gently unfold Amit's arms, Ruchika slipped away, her heart still racing as she glanced back to ensure no one had witnessed their moment. Meanwhile, her parents were eagerly waiting for the newly married couple to get ready, as the "Vidai" ceremony was set for the afternoon, in keeping with Amit's family tradition.

The plan was to shift to their home with all the relatives after the ceremony. Ruchika and Amit hurried to get ready, excitement mingling with nerves as they prepared for the next chapter of their lives. After a hearty breakfast, the family gathered, ready to leave the rented banquet hall together, creating a lively procession filled with laughter, chatter, and the bittersweet emotions that accompanied such a significant transition.

After lunch at Ruchika's home, her sisters gathered around her, helping her prepare for the Vidai ceremony. By 4 PM, she was all set, though her eyes were swollen from crying since the morning. The rituals were completed by 5 PM, and Ruchika, alongside Amit, walked toward the car specially decorated for the bride and groom. A few of Amit's family members had come to take them back.

Ruchika's father was crying even more than her mother, and seeing his tears made Ruchika's heart ache. She couldn't hold back her own tears, feeling a mix of sadness and excitement about leaving her childhood home. As she stepped outside, the familiar fragrance of the Devil's Tree's flowers enveloped her. Ruchika took a long breath, trying to capture the scent in her memory for as long as she could, knowing it was a symbol of her past that would forever be intertwined with her new journey.

As the car began to move, Ruchika took one last glance back at her family, her heart heavy yet filled with hope for the new journey ahead with Amit. The excitement of her new life was tempered by the bittersweet weight of leaving her childhood home behind.

Once they settled into the car, Amit gently took Ruchika's hand, hoping to offer her some comfort. Overwhelmed with emotions, Ruchika couldn't hold back her tears any longer; she leaned her head-on Amit's shoulder, sobbing more loudly than before. His younger brother and one of his cousins, who were also in the car, exchanged concerned glances and tried to console her with light-hearted jokes and warm words, hoping to lift her spirits.

Amit softly reassured her, "You can see your family again tomorrow at the reception. Remember, you can always visit your parents whenever you want. There will be no objections from our side." His words wrapped around her like a warm embrace, reminding Ruchika that her new life didn't mean leaving everything behind. Slowly, her tears began to subside, and she felt a glimmer of comfort in the promise of love and support from her new family.

After 40 minutes, the car finally reached Amit's home where everyone eagerly awaited their arrival. As Ruchika stepped out, she felt a wave of overwhelm wash over her. The faces of Amit's relatives blurred together, even though some had introduced themselves the day before.

A group of elder ladies approached to greet them, gently guiding both Amit and Ruchika out of the car. Another round of rituals began, and Ruchika tried her best to keep up, but exhaustion settled in. The sleepless nights, the anxiety, and the whirlwind of the past few days had taken a toll on her. She wondered when all these rituals would finally end.

Nearly two hours later, she was finally given a moment to breathe. Some of her new relatives kindly suggested she change out of her bridal dress and freshen up. Ruchika felt an immense sense of relief, silently thanking God for this break. For the first time in days, she felt like she might be able to relax, even if just for a moment.

One of her sisters-in-law teased her, saying, "You won't be able to meet your new husband tonight! He can't see your face, as it's part of the marriage ritual." Ruchika felt a wave of relief hearing this. She was thankful that Amit wouldn't come tonight, sparing her from potentially embarrassing situations on their first night together.

Yet, even with that reassurance, she couldn't shake the nervousness about what lay ahead. Thoughts of their "first night" together lingered in her mind, filling her with both curiosity and anxiety. She had no idea what to expect tomorrow after the reception, and the uncertainty kept her on edge. As she prepared to freshen up, Ruchika took a deep breath, trying to gather her thoughts and emotions for the journey ahead.

They led Ruchika into a room and said, "From today, this is your room." As she stepped inside, she couldn't help but notice how large Amit's house was compared to her parents'. The room was spacious and beautifully furnished, with all new furniture—a thoughtful gesture from Amit's family since they hadn't accepted anything from Ruchika's father.

Taking in her new surroundings, her eyes were immediately drawn to the dressing table. She admired its elegant design, especially the three mirrors that allowed her to see all sides while getting ready. It was a small detail, but it made her feel a little more at home in this unfamiliar place. The dressing table, with its beautiful craftsmanship, quickly became her favourite piece in the room, offering a sense of comfort amidst the sea of newness.

After freshening up and changing out of her bridal attire, Ruchika was called for dinner. However, she overheard that she couldn't have her dinner at her in-laws' place tonight. Instead, they took her to a different house for her meal, explaining that this was part of the marriage ritual. She learned that she wasn't allowed to eat at her new home until a specific ritual, which would take place tomorrow, was completed.

At just 23 years old, Ruchika didn't fully understand the significance of all these customs and rituals. She felt overwhelmed but trusted the process and followed whatever instructions were given to her. With little knowledge of the many traditions, she went along, trying her best to adapt to her new life and family.

After returning from dinner, Ruchika noticed that Amit was nowhere to be seen. She assumed he must be sleeping somewhere else for the night. As she headed to her room, she checked the clock and realised it was already 11 o'clock. She remembered that one of her sisters-in-law would be staying with her tonight, as she was new to the family.

When her sister-in-law arrived, Ruchika, feeling completely exhausted from the long day and all the emotions, went to bed. The moment her head touched the pillow, sleep quickly took over, offering her much-needed rest after the whirlwind of wedding rituals. As she drifted off, she hoped for a smoother tomorrow, ready to embrace whatever came next in her new life.

Chapter IV

Ruchika was startled awake by a knocking sound on the door. For a moment, as she opened her eyes, she felt disoriented and confused, unsure of where she was. Then it hit her—she was at her new home. Glancing over, she saw her sister-in-law still asleep, so she quietly got out of bed and opened the door.

To her surprise, Amit stood right in front of her! Ruchika immediately felt shy and a bit flustered at seeing her new husband so early in the morning, especially right after waking up. Amit greeted her with a warm smile, wishing her a good morning before stepping into the room. He casually explained that he was just there to grab his toothbrush and other things.

It suddenly dawned on Ruchika that this was actually Amit's room, and all his belongings were still here. The realisation made her feel even more bashful, but she quickly adjusted, trying to hide her nervousness as Amit moved around the room.

Suddenly, a group of relatives barged into the room, and as soon as they spotted Amit, they burst into laughter. "Bhai, you couldn't even wait till later, huh? You had to see Ruchika first thing in the morning!" they teased; their voices filled with playful mischief. "You waited the whole night just for this moment, didn't you?"

Their laughter filled the room, and Ruchika's face turned bright red. She felt embarrassed, as if she had done something wrong, even though she knew it was all in good fun. The teasing continued, but deep down, she couldn't help but feel shy and flustered. Amit, however, took it in stride, smiling along with his relatives, trying to make Ruchika feel at ease.

As time passed, more rituals took place, especially around lunchtime. One of the important traditions involved Ruchika serving rice to all the elder members of the household, symbolising her role as the new daughter-in-law. She carefully served each elder, feeling a mix of responsibility and nervousness.

After this, Amit approached her with a tray filled with a variety of foods, along with a new saree and jewellery—gifts symbolising his commitment to her. In front of everyone, Amit took an oath, promising to care for her, fulfil his responsibilities, and do everything he could to keep her happy. His words carried warmth and sincerity, making the moment deeply touching.

Ruchika, though shy, felt a sense of comfort and security in this promise. The rituals, though overwhelming, now seemed to hold more meaning as she stepped into this new phase of her life, supported by Amit's vow.

Ruchika began receiving warm attention and affection from everyone in her new family. They showered her with love, making her feel welcomed and cared for. Though she smiled politely and acknowledged their kindness, inside, her heart was filled with a quiet longing. She appreciated the warmth around her but couldn't shake off the bittersweet feeling of leaving her childhood home behind.

As the afternoon rolled on, she found herself caught between the joy of her new life and the nostalgia for the one she had left behind. With each passing moment, Ruchika hoped to find her own place in this new family, yearning to forge bonds that would help ease the transition and fill the void she felt.

Ruchika couldn't help but think of her family and parents. Despite the warmth around her, she eagerly anticipated the evening reception party when she would finally see her loved ones again. The thought of their presence brought her comfort amidst all the newness, and she looked forward to their arrival, hoping it would make her feel more at home.

When the reception began, Ruchika was astonished by its grandeur. Her in-laws had organised a lavish welcome party, transforming an entire ground, as big as a football field, into a fairytale-like setting filled with food stalls and attractions. She was stunned by the elaborate decorations, the twinkling lights, and the lively atmosphere. A raised stage had been set up, where she was asked to sit, allowing her to see everything while receiving congratulations from the guests.

As guests began to arrive to meet and greet her, Ruchika felt overwhelmed. There were so many people all at once, all coming to wish her well in her new life. Amit, along with his brother and father, accompanied her to introduce her to the guests. But after about an hour, Ruchika started to feel suffocated and nervous, lost in the crowd. At just 23, she had never experienced being surrounded by so many unfamiliar faces.

Suddenly, tears began to stream down her cheeks, and she couldn't understand why. The situation felt overwhelming, and she began to wonder why her father had been hesitant about the marriage, thinking that perhaps in this crowd, her identity didn't seem to matter as much.

Somehow, Amit noticed that Ruchika was crying. Worried, he managed to slip away from the guests and hurried over to her. "Are you missing your family? Is something bothering you?" he asked gently. But Ruchika couldn't find the words to explain her feelings. Seeing her so upset in front of everyone made Amit lose his temper. Embarrassed and unsure of how to handle the situation, he began scolding her in front of the guests.

Ruchika, already feeling anxious, became even more panicked and confused by Amit's sudden outburst. Fortunately, some of her sisters-in-law noticed her distress and quickly stepped in. They took her away from the crowd for a while, leading her to their house, which was just beside the field. Outside, Ruchika took a few deep breaths, trying to calm herself as the fresh air began to ease her tension.

After about 15-20 minutes, she agreed to return to the venue, knowing her parents and family would be arriving soon. She didn't want her nervousness to show in front of them, fearing they might panic if they saw her upset.

But one thing became clear to Ruchika—she wasn't going to talk to Amit after how he behaved. If he couldn't understand her feelings in such a vulnerable moment, how could he be expected to understand her for the rest of their life together? The thought left her feeling deeply hurt and disappointed.

As she stepped back into the vibrant atmosphere of the reception, Ruchika couldn't shake off the sting of Amit's words. The laughter and music filled the air, but her heart felt heavy. She longed for the warmth of her family, their familiarity, and the comfort of understanding. Despite being surrounded by people, she felt an increasing distance between her and her new husband. The uncertainty loomed larger than ever, overshadowing the joy of her new beginnings.

Chapter V

After all the guests had left, only a few family members remained. Ruchika's parents arrived, bringing many gifts for her and her new in-laws. The thoughtfulness of the gifts warmed everyone's hearts, and the admiration for her parents' choices helped Ruchika feel calmer and more settled in her new environment.

Amit, on the other hand, realised the mistake he had made with Ruchika. Guilt washed over him for losing his temper in front of everyone, and he approached her several times to apologise. But Ruchika stayed silent, her hurt too deep to be mended so easily. She couldn't find the words to express her feelings, leaving a heavy silence between them.

Now, the last ritual awaited them: preparing Ruchika for the night that marked the beginning of her new journey with Amit. In Indian Bengali tradition, the first night of the bride and groom together after their marriage, commonly referred to as "Suhag Raat," is a special and intimate occasion. It typically follows a series of post-wedding rituals, and while modern practices have blended with traditional customs, certain elements remain deeply rooted in Bengali culture.

The bridal bed, called "*Phool Shojja,*" was traditionally adorned with fresh flowers, usually jasmine or roses, symbolising beauty, romance, and the blossoming of a new relationship. Family members took great care in beautifully arranging the bed, and the fragrance of the flowers set a calming and romantic ambiance.

In traditional Bengali culture, the first night is not just about physical intimacy; it is seen as the beginning of an emotional and spiritual bond. It is a time for the couple to relax after the long wedding ceremonies and get to know each other better. Often, they exchange their first personal conversations as husband and wife.

As Ruchika prepared herself for this significant night, she knew she had no choice but to share it with her husband, Amit. However, when she entered the room, she was taken aback. The bed was exquisitely decorated with fresh flowers, and the soft fragrance filled the air, creating an undeniably romantic atmosphere.

She had heard stories from her married friends about this special night but experiencing it herself felt different. As she stood there, her mind raced back to Amit's sudden first kiss at their house. The memory sent a shiver down her spine, heightening her anxiety and uncertainty about what the night would bring.

Ruchika felt completely exhausted after the long day filled with countless people and rituals. All she wanted was to fall asleep before Amit came into the room. But her brothers-in-law and sisters-in-law lingered, laughing and making light-hearted jokes about the intimate moments she and Amit might share as a new couple. Their teasing, meant to be jovial, only amplified her nerves.

Despite the warm atmosphere and the laughter, Ruchika couldn't shake off the weight of her emotions. The anticipation of the night ahead was a mix of excitement and apprehension, and she wished for just a moment of solitude to collect her thoughts. She felt trapped between her desire to embrace her new life and the hurt that lingered from earlier in the evening.

As the laughter continued, Ruchika took a deep breath, reminding herself that this was a new chapter in her life. No matter the uncertainties, she hoped for a moment of connection with Amit—one that would help bridge the gap created by the earlier misunderstanding. She just needed a little time to adjust, to find her footing in this unfamiliar world.

Their teasing made Ruchika feel incredibly uneasy and shy. She could barely look up as they talked, her face growing warm with embarrassment. The playful banter was unfamiliar, and all she wished for at that moment was a little peace and privacy after such an overwhelming day.

Some of the relatives playfully brought Amit into the room, pushing him onto the bed where Ruchika was sitting. Laughter erupted as they made jokes about the newlyweds who, now being legally married, were expected to be intimate. While the teasing felt light-hearted to them, Ruchika was filled with discomfort.

Inside, she grappled with the reality of arranged marriage. How could society expect her to be close to someone she barely knew, simply because he had put *sindoor* (the symbol of marriage) on her? Ruchika couldn't support this part of the system—the pressure for intimacy with someone she hadn't had time to know, to like, or to fall in love with. It didn't seem fair or right.

To her, true intimacy should only blossom when two people have grown to understand and care for each other deeply, when they naturally feel a connection that draws them closer. How could society overlook such an essential aspect of a relationship? It left

Ruchika questioning the values and expectations imposed upon her, feeling trapped in a system that didn't resonate with her heart.

Ruchika's confusion deepened. She wondered if Amit, her husband, wanted to touch her or be intimate without her consent, what would be the difference between that and assault? Would marriage make it acceptable? The idea horrified her. She couldn't comprehend how society seemed to grant men permission to be physically close to women simply because they were married.

This painful contemplation raised an agonising question in her mind: did marriage transform something wrong into something legal? If a woman wasn't ready, wasn't willing, and was coerced into intimacy, was it any different from an assault? To Ruchika, marriage should be built on mutual respect, understanding, and love—not merely a social contract that automatically conferred one person power over another's body. She felt betrayed by a system that didn't honour a woman's consent, leaving her to question the very foundation of this tradition.

After a few minutes, the relatives finally vacated the room, granting the couple some personal space. Amit got up from the bed, shut the door, and checked all the windows to ensure no one was eavesdropping. He then turned to Ruchika.

"You must be exhausted, Ruchika. I know it's been a long day with so much happening. Please, feel comfortable and go to sleep," Amit said gently. "If you're not comfortable, I can sleep on the sofa."

A wave of relief and gratitude washed over Ruchika at Amit's understanding. His words were kind, and he wasn't pressuring her. She appreciated that he respected her feelings. Quietly, she replied, "You can sleep on the bed. I don't mind. It's your room too."

Amit smiled warmly, respecting her boundaries as he lay down beside her. Without further words, they both found a sense of calm in the shared silence, and Ruchika felt thankful for his patience and sensitivity as they rested after the long, overwhelming day.

As Ruchika stirred awake, she glanced at the clock on the wall. It was 2 o'clock in the morning. She realised that in just four hours, a new day would begin. The thought felt both exciting and daunting, marking the start of her life as a married woman.

Lying there, she couldn't help but reflect on everything that had happened that day: the rituals, the laughter, and the overwhelming emotions. With the quiet of the night enveloping her, she felt a mix of anticipation and nervousness about what tomorrow would bring.

It was the first time Ruchika had to share a bed and a room with someone she barely knew. Even though she felt exhausted, an uneasy tension kept her awake. After about 10-15 minutes, she began to hear Amit's gentle snores, and a smile crept onto her face. It reminded her of her father, who also snored when he was in deep sleep.

With that familiar sound bringing her comfort, Ruchika felt a wave of relaxation wash over her. The warmth of the room and the rhythm of Amit's breathing made her feel a little more at ease. Finally, she closed her eyes, letting go of the day's worries, and within moments, she drifted off to sleep, hoping for a better tomorrow.

Chapter VI

Ruchika slowly opened her eyes and scanned the room, realising she was alone. She glanced at the clock and gasped—it was already 8 AM! She had never slept so deeply before or gotten up this late. Her mother was strict about early mornings, always insisting that she should rise and make tea for everyone in her new home.

Feeling a wave of helplessness wash over her, Ruchika wondered where Amit was. Why hadn't he called her? Just then, she heard the door creak open. Amit walked in, carrying a tray filled with tea and a newspaper.

"Good morning!" he said cheerfully as he entered the room.

Ruchika felt a rush of emotions and didn't know what to say. His easy-going demeanour caught her off guard, and she struggled to find the right words to respond.

"Why didn't you call me when you woke up?" she asked, feeling a mix of concern and curiosity.

Amit smiled and replied, "You were sleeping like a baby! How could I disturb you, darling? I knew you were tired from all the rituals and the many relatives in both our houses, so I thought you needed a good sleep."

Ruchika felt a wave of gratitude for his kindness and consideration. His understanding made her feel more at ease, and she appreciated that he had given her the space to rest after such a long and overwhelming day.

Amit moved closer to Ruchika and gently kissed her forehead. "Get fresh soon," he said softly, "and in the meantime, I'll make some tea for you."

His warm gesture brought a blush to her cheeks, filling her with a mix of surprise and comfort. The simple act of kindness made her heart flutter. As he stepped away to prepare the tea, Ruchika felt a little more at ease, grateful for his thoughtfulness as she gathered her thoughts and prepared to start the day.

She recalled that Amit had lost his mother at a young age, which had shaped much of his life. His father was busy with the business, and Amit worked alongside him to help support their family. She also remembered that Amit's younger brother, who was actually two years older than Ruchika, was still studying.

The realisation struck her: Amit was making tea for both of them. A mix of emotions surged within her. She felt touched by his willingness to take on such small yet significant tasks, but at the same time, it made her reflect on how much responsibility he carried at such a young age. As she got ready, Ruchika couldn't help but feel a growing appreciation for Amit, understanding that they both had their own challenges to face in their new life together.

Quickly getting out of bed, Ruchika hurried to the bathroom, eager to freshen up. Meanwhile, Amit busied himself making tea and reading the newspaper.

After about ten minutes, Ruchika emerged feeling more awake and ready to face the day. She joined Amit at the table, where he had poured two cups of steaming tea. Ruchika was always polite and spoke softly, often waiting for others to initiate conversation. She hoped Amit would have something to say.

Amit looked up from the newspaper and smiled at her. "Ruchika, please feel free to make yourself at home. This is now your home too. After you finish your tea, I'd like you to meet my father."

Ruchika nodded, feeling a mix of warmth and nervousness at his words. She appreciated his kindness and the invitation to feel comfortable in their new space, but the thought of meeting his father made her heart race.

After finishing the tea, Ruchika and Amit headed towards his father's room. Ruchika took a deep breath and walked towards her father-in-law's room, knocking softly on the door, seeking permission to enter. Once she heard his gentle "come in," she opened the door and stepped inside.

The room was much larger and more elaborately decorated than hers, filled with rich colours and elegant furnishings. Ruchika felt a mixture of awe and nervousness as she greeted her father-in-law with a warm smile.

"Good morning, Papa. Would you like a cup of tea?" she asked politely.

Her father-in-law returned her smile and replied, "Thank you, Ruchika, but I've already had my tea."

He then informed her that she and Amit would be visiting her home soon for some additional rituals, as her father had confirmed this during last night's events. Ruchika nodded, feeling both excited and apprehensive about the upcoming visit, knowing it would be another step in her new life.

As she stepped out of her father-in-law's room and made her way back to her own, Ruchika felt a bit uncertain about what to do next. Walking through the house, she encountered some relatives who had been there the night before. One of the ladies approached her with a warm smile.

"How was your first night with Amit?" she asked playfully, a hint of mischief in her eyes.

Ruchika felt her cheeks heat up at the question. She wasn't quite sure how to respond, caught off guard by the light-heartedness of the inquiry. "It was… different," she finally managed to say, trying to keep her tone polite while feeling a wave of shyness wash over her.

The lady laughed softly, noticing Ruchika's discomfort. "That's a good way to put it! Just remember, every relationship takes time to grow. You'll find your rhythm together."

Ruchika nodded, grateful for the woman's reassurance. As she walked away, she felt a mixture of relief and lingering anxiety. With so many changes happening so quickly, she hoped that with time, she and Amit would find their way. The thought of their future together both excited and frightened her, but she was determined to approach it with an open heart and mind.

The lady laughed softly, sensing Ruchika's unease. "Don't worry; it takes time to adjust. Just be yourself." With that, she offered a reassuring smile before continuing on her way. Ruchika felt a mix of relief and nervousness but appreciated the kindness behind the words.

As Ruchika tried to gather her thoughts, more relatives approached her, eager to ask about her experience from the night before. Feeling uneasy with their questions, she simply replied, "I slept well last night."

However, one of her sisters-in-law burst into laughter, pointing at the other relatives with a playful grin. "Why, Ruchika? How can you sleep? *Phool sojja* (the flower bed) is not meant for sleeping! Don't you like my brother?"

Ruchika felt her face flush with embarrassment at the teasing. She couldn't help but glance down, her heart racing as she tried to compose herself. The light-hearted banter was meant to be fun, but it only made her feel more self-conscious about the intimacy that everyone seemed to expect between her and Amit. She smiled awkwardly, wishing the ground would open up and swallow her whole.

Just as Ruchika felt overwhelmed by the teasing, Amit appeared, sensing her discomfort. He swiftly made his way through the group, a determined look on his face.

"Hey, what's going on here?" he asked, his voice firm yet light-hearted. He gently caught Ruchika by the arm and pulled her slightly closer to him, shielding her from the playful antics of his mischievous siblings.

"Come on, everyone! Give her a break. It's her first day here," Amit said, flashing a smile at the relatives. "Let's not bombard her with questions."

His protective gesture made Ruchika feel a rush of relief and gratitude. She glanced up at him, thankful for his timely intervention. The group chuckled, appreciating Amit's efforts to rescue his new bride from their playful teasing. Ruchika felt a little more at ease, knowing that Amit was there to support her amidst the lively chaos.

As the day went on, it was filled with laughter and chatter. Relatives gathered around, excitedly checking the gifts that had arrived from Ruchika's home, showering her with compliments about her parents' thoughtful choices. They began to unwrap the gifts she had received during the celebrations, and Ruchika's eyes widened in amazement.

She had never seen so many gifts in one place before; the room was overflowing with colourful boxes and beautifully wrapped presents. Each item seemed to tell a story, filled with love and good wishes from family and friends.

After lunch, the house began to quiet down as most of the relatives departed, leaving just a few behind. Now, only Amit, Ruchika, her father-in-law, her brother-in-law, and two maids remained in the home. Ruchika felt a sense of calm wash over her as the lively atmosphere settled, making the house feel more like a place she could call home.

As night fell, Ruchika felt the familiar flutter of nerves return. The thought of what might happen that evening weighed heavily on her mind. She recalled how Amit had respected her boundaries the night before and wondered if tonight would be different.

However, she was pleasantly surprised when Amit returned to their room after they had dinner together. He approached her with a gentle smile, kissing her forehead affectionately. "You should sleep early tonight, darling," he said softly. "We need to wake up early tomorrow to go to your home for the further marriage ritual."

Ruchika felt a wave of relief wash over her. Amit's thoughtful demeanour reassured her that he was considerate of her feelings. Grateful for his understanding, she nodded and settled into bed, feeling more at ease as she prepared for the upcoming day.

As Ruchika settled into bed, she soon began to hear Amit's soft snoring from across the room. A smile crept onto her face at the sound; it reminded her of home and the comforting familiarity of shared spaces.

Feeling relaxed and safe, she allowed herself to drift off to sleep, grateful for the warmth of the day and the gentle presence of Amit beside her. With her worries slowly fading away, Ruchika fell into a peaceful slumber, ready to embrace whatever tomorrow would bring.

Chapter VII

The next morning, Ruchika woke up at her usual time, around 6 AM. After freshening up, she headed to the kitchen, eager to make tea for everyone, just as her mother had taught her before her marriage. She first served tea to her father-in-law, who was just waking up. He smiled and reminded her to get ready since they would be heading to her parents' house soon.

Noticing that her brother-in-law Rahul was still asleep, Ruchika returned to her room with a tray containing two cups of tea. As she entered, she found Amit still in bed, not yet awake. She hesitated for a moment, unsure whether it would be appropriate to call him. Just then, Amit stirred, his eyes meeting hers.

The moment their eyes locked, a shy smile spread across Ruchika's face. "You should wake up; we have to go," she said softly.

Amit smiled back at her, a playful glint in his eyes. "So, madam, you're ready to go to your home? I hope you had a good sleep," he teased, enjoying the light banter.

Ruchika could only nod, feeling a rush of warmth and shyness at his words. The playful exchange eased her nerves, making her feel more comfortable in this new chapter of her life.

By 10 a.m., Amit and Ruchika arrived at her parents' home for the pooja that was arranged as part of the post-marriage rituals. Some relatives were already gathered, ready to join the ceremony and offer their blessings to the newly married couple.

As they approached the entrance, Ruchika was immediately greeted by the familiar, soothing fragrance of the devil's tree blossoms. She inhaled deeply, feeling a sense of warmth and nostalgia fill her heart. Noticing the sweet scent, Amit smiled and asked curiously, "What a beautiful fragrance! Did your family do something special for their new son-in-law?"

Ruchika smiled at his playful question and pointed towards the blooming tree in the garden. "The fragrance comes from the devil's tree blossoms," she explained gently. Amit looked at the tree with admiration, nodding in appreciation. "So, this is what makes your home so welcoming," he said with a grin. Ruchika felt a deep sense of joy, knowing that her home had embraced him just as warmly as he had embraced her new life with him.

After the pooja and rituals were completed by 11:30 a.m., Ruchika found herself surrounded by her cousin sisters and sisters-in-law who wasted no time teasing her. They giggled and asked her all sorts of playful questions about her *"phool sajja"* night, eager to know how Amit had shown his love and affection.

Ruchika felt her cheeks flush with embarrassment as the questions kept coming. She tried to smile and laugh along, but inside, she felt a bit overwhelmed. The teasing was light-hearted, but it left her unsure of how to respond, especially when they started asking about her honeymoon plans.

"Where are you going for your honeymoon? Have you decided yet?" one of them asked with a mischievous smile.

Ruchika had no idea what to say. There hadn't been any conversation between her and Amit about their honeymoon, and she wasn't sure how to explain that. She shifted in her seat, her mind racing for an answer, but all she could do was give a shy smile and try to steer the conversation in another direction. She hoped the teasing would end soon, but despite her discomfort, she knew it was all in good fun.

Just a few minutes later, Amit appeared and noticed the teasing Ruchika was enduring. With a playful grin, he asked his sisters-in-law, "Why are you all troubling my bride just to have some fun?"

The group burst into laughter, one of them teasing, "Bhaiya, it seems like you can't even leave Ruchika alone for a few minutes without missing her, right?"

Amit laughed along with them, making a few light-hearted jokes himself, which made everyone feel even more at ease. Ruchika, meanwhile, could feel her cheeks flush as she blushed at the attention, but she smiled warmly, appreciating how Amit was handling the teasing with charm.

Then one of his sisters asked, "So, bhaiya, where are you taking Ruchika for your honeymoon, and when?"

Without missing a beat, Amit replied with a mischievous grin, "Why don't you ask your sister if she'll let me go with her? She's still nervous about sleeping in the same room with me!"

Everyone erupted into laughter at Amit's playful response, and even Ruchika couldn't help but smile despite her embarrassment. The room filled with warmth and laughter, and she realised how fortunate she was to have someone who could handle these moments with such light-heartedness.

Suddenly, Ruchika heard her mother calling her from the other room, and she seized the opportunity to escape the teasing and awkwardness. Grateful for the distraction, she quickly excused herself and went to see her mother. Ruchika's mother, a middle-aged homemaker, greeted her with warmth and familiarity. She knew her daughter well and had a series of questions ready, eager to know how Ruchika was adjusting to her new life.

"How are your in-laws? Are they treating you well? And how is Amit's behaviour?" her mother asked with genuine concern.

Ruchika answered her mother's questions one by one, feeling comforted by the familiarity of their conversation. But then, as the questions continued, her mother surprised her by asking, "And... has Amit been intimate with you yet in these 2-3 days?"

Ruchika's face turned red with embarrassment. She hadn't expected even her own mother to ask such a personal question. It seemed like everyone was curious about the same thing, and it made her feel even more awkward. She lowered her gaze, unsure of how to respond, feeling both shy and uncomfortable. The thought that even her mother, who usually understood her so well, had joined in with the others made her feel vulnerable.

That night, feeling overwhelmed and seeking comfort, Ruchika went to her mother and quietly asked, almost nagging, if she could sleep with her instead of going back to her room. She longed for the familiar warmth and safety of her mother's presence. However, her mother gently shook her head, understanding the deeper implications of her daughter's request.

"No, Ruchika," her mother said softly, "Amit is in a new place, unfamiliar with your home. It's your responsibility to make him feel comfortable. If you stay with me, it might hurt his feelings. You have to make him feel welcome."

Though Ruchika didn't agree with her mother's perspective, feeling unsure about her own role in this new life, she knew she had no choice. With a reluctant sigh, she made her way back to her room, where Amit was already waiting for her.

As she entered, Amit looked up, his face lighting up with a gentle smile. He had been patiently waiting for her return, and though Ruchika still felt unsure and hesitant, his warmth made her feel a little less uneasy. She silently prepared for bed, knowing this was just another step in the long journey of getting to know her husband and finding her place in this new chapter of life.

Amit gently asked Ruchika, "Can we go to the terrace now, if you don't mind?"

Ruchika's face lit up with joy at the idea. She had always loved the calm of a quiet night, and the thought of spending time on the terrace with Amit made her feel a sudden rush of excitement. Smiling, she replied, "Why not? Everyone is almost asleep now; we can go easily."

Amit chuckled softly at her response and teasingly said, "Relax, Ruchi. We're a married couple now. You don't have to worry that anyone will say anything. We can go anywhere together; no one will scold you."

Ruchika felt her cheeks flush with embarrassment at Amit's playful words. She hadn't realised how deeply ingrained her habit of seeking approval still was, even in such a simple situation. Amit's relaxed and reassuring tone made her feel a little shy, but it also comforted her. She smiled back at him, feeling grateful that he was helping her adjust to this new reality where they were no longer just strangers but partners, free to be themselves.

Chapter VIII

—⚜—

Ruchika and Amit walked up to the terrace, where the night air felt cool and calm. Under the soft glow of the full moon, Ruchika noticed an old swing. It looked worn but inviting. She walked over, sat on it, and her smile grew wide, like a little girl who had just found her lost treasure. The gentle sway of the swing filled her heart with joy, making her feel free, as if all her worries had melted away.

The atmosphere was truly romantic. The full moon bathed everything in silver light, while the sweet smell of the devil's tree blossoms filled the air, making the night feel like a dream. Amit, feeling the magic of the moment, began to hum a gentle tune. He then asked softly, "Ruchi, can you sing a song for me? I love hearing you sing."

Ruchika blushed but nodded. She took a deep breath and began singing a lovely Rabindra Sangeet, "*Sedin dujone dule chilu bone, phoolo dore badha jhulona…*" ("That day, we swayed together in the grove, On a swing adorned with garlands of flowers.")

Amit listened, captivated by her sweet voice. He moved closer to her, gently pushing the swing as they swayed together under the moonlight. The whole scene felt like a warm hug from the universe, a perfect moment just for them, two souls drawn together by new love and a shared silence that spoke louder than words.

Since morning, Amit had started calling her "Ruchi" instead of Ruchika. She loved the way he said it, a soft nickname that made her feel special. It felt like he was getting closer to her, and that small change in how he addressed her warmed her heart.

They spent some time talking about their hopes and dreams, sharing stories from their childhoods, and finding joy in the simple pleasure of each other's company. Ruchika felt her walls slowly coming down, allowing herself to be more open and vulnerable.

As they continued to talk, Ruchika sensed a growing comfort between them. The playful banter from earlier seemed like a distant memory, replaced by a deeper connection. She realised that the path ahead might still be uncertain, but in this moment, everything felt right.

Apart from her studies, Ruchika was known for her singing and painting. These talents defined her, and now, as she shared her voice with Amit, she felt a new connection blossoming between them.

Both felt completely at ease on the terrace, surrounded by the lovely scent of the devil tree blossoms. It was the perfect setting for two hearts growing closer. It seemed like the world outside had disappeared, leaving just the two of them in this tender moment.

Amit gently pulled Ruchika closer, and she instinctively knew what was coming. Her heart raced as she closed her eyes, giving in to the moment. Amit wrapped his arms around her, holding her close. He softly kissed her forehead, then her eyes, her cheeks, and finally her lips, before moving down to her neck.

Ruchika felt herself melting in his embrace, her emotions swirling with the warmth of his touch. She wrapped her arms around Amit's neck, holding him tight as they lost themselves in the tenderness of the moment, their love quietly growing under the moonlit sky. The moon, radiant and serene, and the enchanting fragrance of the Devil Tree's blossoms stood as silent witnesses to the couple's beautiful moment, a scene etched in nature's timeless embrace.

Suddenly, their romantic moment was interrupted by music playing nearby. Startled but curious, Amit and Ruchika opened their eyes. They saw a group of Ruchika's brothers and sisters on the terrace, grinning and holding a tape recorder that played a cheerful tune. Laughter and celebration filled the air.

Her siblings clapped and teased, congratulating Amit with playful remarks. Ruchika blushed deeply, feeling embarrassed yet amused by the surprise. Amit smiled at the joyful chaos. The quiet moment turned into a lively celebration, with her family joining in to make it even more memorable.

They started playing around on the terrace, laughter filling the night as Ruchika's siblings eagerly asked about their honeymoon plans. Ruchika, feeling a warm affection for Amit, gently suggested, "What if we go to a hill station?"

Amit grinned, replying with excitement, "Sure, why not!"

Everyone erupted into cheers and shouts of joy, celebrating the couple's bond and the idea of their first trip together as newlyweds. The atmosphere buzzed with laughter, love, and adventure, making Ruchika feel even more at home in her new life with Amit.

After the lively celebration, everyone eventually went to bed, but Amit found a way to stay close to Ruchika. As they settled down, he wrapped his arms around her, holding her tightly. The warmth of his embrace was comforting, and Ruchika felt his affection.

Amit kissed her deeply, his lips showing all the tenderness he felt. Ruchika melted into his arms, giving herself to the moment. As they shared this intimacy, she felt a mix of excitement and peace, finally allowing herself to relax.

Before long, the gentle sound of Amit's heartbeat lulled Ruchika into a peaceful sleep, her head resting on his chest, holding him close as she surrendered to the bliss of the night.

Chapter IX

Ruchika and Amit woke up late, around 8 o'clock in the morning. Ruchika felt a bit embarrassed because she knew her family usually got up early. She quickly got out of bed, wanting to make tea for everyone.

As she stepped into the kitchen, she was surprised to see her mother standing there, smiling brightly. Her mother handed her a tray with two cups of steaming tea.

Ruchika was confused. "You're not upset that I woke up late?" she asked, wondering why her mother seemed so happy.

Her mother shook her head, still smiling. "Not at all! You just got married, so it's okay to sleep in a little," she said warmly.

Ruchika couldn't believe it. Was this new kindness because she was now a married woman? A smile spread across her face as she took the tray, feeling grateful for her mother's understanding. This new chapter in her life seemed to bring a fresh sense of joy and warmth to her family.

Ruchika understood that some events in life have the power to change everything around us. Getting married was one of those moments. It not only marked a new chapter in her life but also transformed how her family interacted with her. She felt a deeper connection with her loved ones, and their support felt even more significant now that she had taken this important step.

Just after finishing their tea, Amit received a call from his father. There were urgent issues at the office that needed his attention, and he was asked to come back soon. Ruchika felt a wave of disappointment wash over her. She had hoped they would spend three full days together, but this sudden change in plans left her feeling sad.

Amit tried to comfort her, saying, "You can stay with your family, Ruchi. I'll come back to pick you up tomorrow." Though she agreed, her heart felt heavy at the thought of him leaving so soon.

When Ruchika's parents heard about the change in plans, they quickly intervened. They expressed their concern, saying it wasn't proper for Ruchika to stay alone, especially right after the wedding. They insisted that Amit should return home with her and suggested they stick together as a couple.

Ruchika felt a mix of emotions—she appreciated their care but was also frustrated by the restrictions. Still, she knew the importance of following traditions, so she agreed to return home with Amit. As they prepared to leave, she tried to focus on the moments they had shared rather than the ones they were losing.

After breakfast, Ruchika's mother asked Amit, "Son, when will Ruchika be able to return to college? Will it be after your honeymoon, or can she go back sooner?"

"I'll let you know, Mom," Amit replied. "We haven't planned the honeymoon yet."

Ruchika's father, feeling a bit irritated, chimed in as he noticed the rush to get going. "Why are you worried about her college? She's a bright student; she'll manage. Let them enjoy a few more days together, and then she can start going back."

But Ruchika's mother was concerned. "If she doesn't return soon, it will be hard for her to catch up. She should get back to her studies as soon as possible."

She couldn't shake her worry that Ruchika might miss out on important lessons. Although she knew Ruchika's in-laws were well-off, she dreamed of her daughter standing on her own two feet, independent and self-sufficient, rather than relying on anyone else.

Amit, being a thoughtful person, understood Ruchika's mother's concerns and wanted to ease the tension between her and her husband. "I'll talk to my father as soon as we get back," he said. "I'll make sure we arrange for Ruchika to join her college soon."

His calm response helped to settle the atmosphere at the table, reassuring both Ruchika's parents that he was taking their worries seriously.

After breakfast, Ruchika and Amit returned to their home, ready to begin this new chapter in their lives together.

Chapter X

After Amit dropped Ruchika off at her in-laws' home, he headed straight to the office. When Ruchika arrived, she found no one at home except for two maids who politely asked if she needed anything. She declined, having already had breakfast at her parents' house. This time, she had brought all her books with her, eager to return to college and start studying again.

During lunch, Ruchika ate alone in the empty house. She noticed how smoothly everything ran. Three or four servants managed the household, all working without needing instructions. This surprised Ruchika, as her mother usually directed everything at her parents' home. She thought to herself that even if the maids asked her what to do, she wouldn't know how to respond. After finishing lunch, she felt a bit tired and decided to take a nap.

Around 5 p.m., she was awakened by some noise outside her room. Curious, she opened the bedroom door to see what was happening and found her father-in-law sitting at the dining table, being served food by the servants. Ruchika was surprised to see him having lunch so late! She suddenly remembered her father once telling her that there are many differences between a business family and a family with regular jobs.

Feeling she should be present to assist her father-in-law, she approached him and stood nearby. She noticed he seemed a bit upset, perhaps due to a work issue. Gently, she asked if he needed anything. He smiled warmly at her and asked about her parents. Ruchika replied that they were doing well and remained standing until he finished his meal.

One of the servants asked Ruchika if she would like some tea, and since she did, she said yes. After enjoying her tea, she returned to her books, as there wasn't much else to do.

Around 6 p.m., one of her mother-in-law's relatives visited Ruchika, curious about why she came back early from her parents' house. Ruchika knew that the entire four-story building was occupied by her father-in-law's brothers and their families, each living on their own floor. Seeing this relative brought Ruchika some happiness, as she finally had someone to talk to after spending the whole day alone.

They enjoyed each other's company, and the relative shared a touching story about how Amit's mother passed away at a young age and how the family came together to care for both brothers after her death. Hearing this sad story made Ruchika feel a deep sense of sympathy for them. After about an hour, her relative left, and Ruchika waited for Amit to return. In the meantime, she wondered if she might see her brother-in-law, who could be back from college soon.

Amit returned home around 8 p.m., looking tired and visibly disturbed. Ruchika knew she shouldn't ask him anything until he was ready to share what was on his mind. Instead, she gently offered to make him some tea or coffee. Amit politely declined, saying he'd prefer an early dinner since he hadn't had time to eat lunch. Ruchika was surprised—how could someone work the entire day with just breakfast? This made her realise how tough and demanding their routine was because of their business, and she couldn't help but feel concerned about the strain it placed on them.

After dinner, Ruchika noticed that Amit went to his father's room, where they talked for about half an hour. She suspected their conversation was related to business. Suddenly, she heard Amit's father shouting at him, and it was clear they were having an argument. This made Ruchika feel uneasy, as she had never been comfortable around her father-in-law. Hearing him shout now scared her, especially since she had never seen her own father raise his voice at anyone. The tension in the house made her feel unsettled, and she wished she could do something to ease the situation.

Feeling unsure of what to do, Ruchika quietly waited for Amit to return to their room. Her mind was filled with worry, but she knew that stepping in might not help. All she could do was hope that the argument would end soon, and that Amit would come back to her, where she could offer him some comfort and support. The waiting felt long, and her heart raced with unease, but she stayed patient, knowing Amit would share when he was ready.

After a while, Amit finally came into the room where Ruchika was waiting. She noticed right away that he was still very angry and didn't say a word to her. Unsure of what to do or say, Ruchika gently asked if he needed anything. Amit responded that he just wanted to sleep early because he was in a bad mood.

Ruchika understood that Amit didn't want to share his problems with her, and this made her feel helpless. She wished she could help but knew he needed space. As they lay down to sleep, Amit fell asleep quickly, but Ruchika remained awake for a long time, her mind filled with worry and sadness, unable to shake the feeling of being shut out.

Ruchika felt deeply confused, wondering if the gap in their ages—she being six years younger than Amit—might be affecting their relationship. She believed that friendship is the foundation of a strong bond, and right now, she felt distant from Amit. The way he shut her out, especially during difficult moments, left her feeling unsure of how to connect with him. She began to question whether their age difference was making it harder for them to communicate openly and support each other as equals in the relationship.

Chapter XI

The next morning, Ruchika woke up late, feeling exhausted from her restless night. When she didn't see Amit in the room, she quickly freshened up and stepped out to find him waiting for her with a cup of tea. Amit smiled at her, asking how she had slept and apologising for not talking to her the night before because he was upset. Ruchika felt relieved by his warm gesture and asked about his plans for the day.

"Ruchi," Amit began gently, "you must have been surprised by what happened with my father last night. I went to talk to him about your college plans, but he doesn't want you to continue studying now that you are part of our family. According to him, once you're married, further education or even working outside the home is not acceptable. It's a family rule."

Ruchika listened intently as Amit continued, his voice filled with regret. "I know how much your parents want you to complete your studies. It was my mistake not to discuss this before our marriage. Your father already had reservations about us, and if I had told him, you wouldn't be able to pursue your education afterward; he would never have agreed to it. I thought after we got married, I could convince my father to let you continue, but I'm so sorry, Ruchi. My father won't budge on this."

Ruchika felt a mix of emotions—shock, disappointment, and sadness. She understood Amit's struggle, but the weight of the situation began to sink in as she processed this unexpected barrier to her dreams. She felt torn, unsure of how to break this news to her parents. She knew they'd be deeply upset, and the thought of disappointing them weighed heavily on her mind. All day, she found herself lost in thought, unable to focus on anything.

In the evening, Amit came home early and suggested they go out together, trying to lift her spirits. But Ruchika, still feeling low, politely refused. Amit understood immediately; he knew the pain of unfulfilled dreams all too well. He, too, had once wanted to study abroad and follow his own path, but his father's pressure forced him to give up on those dreams and join the family business instead.

Seeing Ruchika in this situation brought back memories of his own struggles, and he silently shared in her disappointment, wishing he could change things for both of them. After dinner, Amit gently asked Ruchika to join him on the terrace. She followed silently, still overwhelmed by everything. As they stood under the night sky, Amit spoke softly, promising that he would talk to her parents about the situation. He tried his best to cheer her up, but Ruchika, unable to hold back her emotions any longer, suddenly burst into tears. Amit felt helpless, unsure of how to ease her pain.

The sky above them glowed with the moon and a blanket of stars, as if they were silently witnessing this fragile moment. Amit pulled Ruchika close, holding her tightly. He cupped her face in his hands, kissed her softly, and wiped away her tears with his lips. In that tender moment, he whispered comforting words: "Ruchi, I will do everything I can to help you. I promise. I know this is hard... I lost my mother when I was young, and sometimes I think if she were here, she would have fought for you. She was a strong, noble woman, but even she wasn't allowed to work by my father."

Amit's words carried a deep sense of understanding, and as he held her close, Ruchika felt a small glimmer of comfort, knowing he was trying to support her in the best way he could.

From that day forward, Ruchika found it hard to support or respect her father-in-law. His rigid mindset and his opposition to her continuing her education made her see him as controlling and dominating. To Ruchika, he represented someone who was against women's growth and development. This realisation created a growing distance between them. She struggled with the fact that, in his eyes, her dreams and ambitions didn't matter simply because she was a woman, leaving her feeling trapped and resentful.

Ruchika found it hard to believe that, even in the 21st century, her father-in-law held such orthodox views. His resistance to her education and independence felt outdated and out of place in a world where women were encouraged to pursue their dreams. This made it even harder for her to connect with him, as she felt stifled by his traditional mindset. Ruchika couldn't help but feel frustrated, wondering how someone could still hold such rigid beliefs about a woman's role in society.

After a month, Amit planned their honeymoon to Kullu-Manali. During this time, Ruchika and Amit grew even closer, developing a beautiful bond filled with understanding. Ruchika felt confident that Amit loved her wholeheartedly. They visited Ruchika's parents, although they didn't stay the night. Amit took the opportunity to speak with Ruchika's father about his father's decision regarding her education. Ruchika's parents were understandably upset; they wanted the best for their daughter but felt powerless in this situation. In India, once a daughter is given to another family, her parents often feel they can't intervene or force any changes in her new life.

Ruchika's mother expressed her frustration, asking why Amit hadn't discussed this issue before their marriage. This question weighed heavily on Amit, as he knew the importance of honesty and communication in relationships. Ruchika sensed the tension in the room but felt grateful for her parents' support, knowing they cared deeply for her future.

During their honeymoon, Ruchika found herself surrounded by the breathtaking beauty of Kullu-Manali. The stunning landscapes and serene atmosphere created a magical backdrop for her and Amit. Here, she experienced a profound connection with Amit, whose caring and loving nature made her heart swell with happiness. As they explored the picturesque surroundings together, Ruchika felt a deep sense of gratitude for having Amit as her life partner. She realised how blessed she was to share this moment with someone who understood and supported her. In this heavenly setting, Ruchika opened her heart completely to Amit, cherishing every moment spent together. Their love blossomed amidst the natural beauty, and she felt more connected to him than ever before, embracing the joy and intimacy of their relationship.

Now, Ruchika felt comfortable sharing everything with Amit without hesitation. One day, as they enjoyed each other's company, she asked him if they could buy a devil tree for their home. However, Amit expressed his disappointment, explaining that there wasn't enough space for such a tree in their house. Ruchika felt a little disheartened by his response, as she had hoped to add a unique touch to their home with the tree. Still, she appreciated Amit's honesty and understood the practical concerns of their living situation. This moment highlighted their growing bond, where Ruchika could express her desires, and Amit could share his thoughts openly, even if it led to a small disagreement.

Chapter XII

It's been two years since Ruchika moved into her in-laws' house, and she was genuinely happy there. Everyone in the family loved her, and she had taken on many responsibilities, managing the household with grace. She had also started her own boutique business, which she ran successfully.

However, recently, both her family and in-laws started pressuring her to have a child. But Amit, her husband, wasn't ready. He had just started his own business after leaving his father's company, where he faced several challenges. Amit had partnered with his friend Aniruddha, and together they worked hard to make their new venture a success.

Ruchika also took it upon herself to find a bride for her brother-in-law. With Amit being so busy, she found herself spending a lot of time alone. Amit's new office was located in Aniruddha's building, so Ruchika often met Aniruddha. He was charming and well-mannered, and they developed a good friendship. Aniruddha's home was an old heritage building, and whenever Ruchika visited, she always met his parents, who were warm and welcoming. They appreciated her kindness, and Ruchika felt a connection to their home, which was surrounded by devil trees, giving the place a mysterious yet inviting atmosphere.

Amit trusted Aniruddha completely. On days when Amit couldn't accompany Ruchika to events or social gatherings, he would often ask Aniruddha to go with her. Ruchika felt comfortable around Aniruddha and admired his intelligence and warmth.

As time went on, the pressure to start a family became more intense. Ruchika struggled with this, feeling torn between her own desires and the expectations of both families. Amit was focused on his business, and his commitment to work grew even deeper after some struggles with his father's company. While Ruchika tried to embrace her role as the *"bari bahu"* (eldest daughter-in-law), her personal dreams often took a backseat.

One day, after another year had passed, Ruchika discovered she was pregnant. Both families were overjoyed, but there were complications in her pregnancy, and the doctor advised her to take it easy. After nine months, she gave birth to a healthy baby boy, bringing immense happiness to everyone, especially Amit.

Amit's business also picked up after the baby's arrival, and he became busier than ever. He had to hire more employees to keep up with the growing workload. Meanwhile, Ruchika was fully immersed in caring for her newborn and managing her boutique, which had slowed down during her pregnancy. She was determined to revive it now that things were stabilising.

Even though everything seemed perfect from the outside, Ruchika and Amit barely spent time together. Their lives had become so hectic that they drifted into separate worlds. Amit was always at work, and Ruchika's priority was their baby. While they loved each other, the connection they once shared was fading, and they weren't addressing the emotional gap that was growing between them.

Aniruddha became a frequent visitor to their home, often playing with the baby when Amit was busy. He had formed a close bond with their family. Ruchika noticed that Aniruddha, despite his friendly demeanour, was lonely. His marriage hadn't worked out, and his wife had moved to another city for her career. Though Aniruddha never talked much about it, Ruchika sensed his sadness, and she couldn't help but feel a soft spot for him.

Amit often came home late, and by that time, Ruchika was already asleep with the baby. They hardly shared a moment together anymore, and Ruchika didn't mind. She knew the servants would take care of Amit when he came home. But somewhere deep down, she felt the distance growing between them.

Ruchika's life was filled with love for her baby and her duties as a wife and daughter-in-law, but her personal dreams and emotional needs were quietly being set aside. Her budding friendship with Aniruddha made her feel supported, especially on the days when Amit was absent. Aniruddha's presence was comforting, and the bond they shared became a source of strength for Ruchika as she navigated the challenges of motherhood.

While Ruchika trusted that things would get better with Amit once the baby grew older, she also realised that something was missing between them. They needed to reconnect emotionally, but both were too busy to acknowledge the gap. Ruchika believed in their love but knew that without communication and effort from both sides, it would be hard to bridge the distance that had quietly crept into their marriage.

Chapter XIII

A new chapter began in Ruchika's life when Amit's brother got married, and his new wife joined their family. Despite being younger, Ruchika quickly formed a sisterly bond with her because of her warmth and kindness.

One day, Ruchika's father-in-law called her into his room. She hesitated because she had been avoiding him due to his behaviour, but she went in anyway. His words shocked her— he accused her of being unaware of what was happening at home and told her that Amit was having an affair. Ruchika felt like her world was falling apart.

She couldn't bring herself to confront Amit directly, but she had noticed that he had become distant. Desperate and confused, she rushed to Amit's brother and shared what she had heard. He comforted her, suggesting that it must be a misunderstanding, but Ruchika still felt lost.

That evening, Ruchika quietly followed Amit to the terrace. From a distance, she overheard him speaking softly on the phone with a woman, his tone gentle and calm. Her heart sank. When she returned to her room, she felt overwhelmed and trapped, unable to share her pain with anyone—not even her parents. The truth felt too heavy to bear, leaving Ruchika to carry it alone.

Suddenly, an idea came to her—she decided to talk to Aniruddha, Amit's best friend and business partner. Aniruddha often visited, especially since he adored their little one. Ruchika trusted him and thought he might know something about Amit's behaviour. She believed he could help her understand what was really going on.

However, Ruchika knew she had to handle this carefully. If Amit found out she was asking questions behind his back, especially through his closest friend, it could make things worse. So, she planned to speak with Aniruddha privately, away from prying eyes. She waited for the right moment, and after weeks, the opportunity finally came when Amit left for a business trip for a few days. Aniruddha, who wasn't going with him, was still in town. This was her chance.

Without hesitation, Ruchika called Aniruddha and asked if he could meet her. Aniruddha was surprised by her urgency, wondering why she couldn't meet at Amit's place. Ruchika explained that it was a personal matter that couldn't be discussed at home. The seriousness in her voice convinced him, and he agreed to meet her at his place after office hours.

At 7 o'clock that evening, Ruchika arrived at Aniruddha's home. The sweet aroma of blooming devil trees filled the air, making the evening feel almost magical. It was the month of October. It reminded her that she hadn't gone out by herself at night since her baby was born. Tonight, she made an exception, taking a cab to keep her meeting a secret.

As she sat in Aniruddha's living room, the weight of what she was about to discuss pressed heavily on her. Aniruddha watched her with concern, sensing her troubled thoughts. He offered her a drink to help her relax, and though she didn't usually drink, she accepted, hoping it might ease her nerves. As time passed, the music and soft lighting created a comforting atmosphere, helping her feel more at ease.

Aniruddha gently asked, "What's troubling you? You seem so worried."

Ruchika hesitated for a moment, then said, "Promise me you'll tell me the truth, and whatever we talk about stays between us."

Aniruddha assured her, "I promise."

Taking a deep breath, Ruchika told him what her father-in-law had said about Amit. Then, she asked, "You spend almost the whole day with Amit. You know where he goes and who he meets. Can you tell me if he's having an affair… and who she is, if that's true?"

Aniruddha looked at Ruchika, processing her words. After a pause, he gently responded, "I don't think what you've heard is true. If something like that was happening, I would have noticed. But since you mentioned it, I'll pay closer attention."

Seeing her distress, Aniruddha softly added, "Come here." After years of friendship, he felt it was right to offer her a comforting hug, hoping to calm her troubled heart.

Ruchika, affected by the drinks and her emotions, moved closer to Aniruddha. Though he was married, he had been living apart from his wife for three years, and like Ruchika, he longed for emotional warmth. In that moment, both Ruchika and Aniruddha sought comfort in each other's presence.

Lost in the embrace, Ruchika felt overwhelmed by everything—the baby, her work, the strain of family life, and the growing distance from Amit. The lack of intimacy in her life had drained her, and she surrendered to the exhaustion. For Aniruddha, who had always admired her kindness, this moment felt like a release from his own loneliness.

But just as Ruchika began to give in to the moment, a sudden realisation hit her. She pushed Aniruddha away. She couldn't let herself cross this line. Despite everything, she loved Amit, and she was a mother now. With a heavy heart, she said, "I can't do this, Aniruddha. I'm sorry… I need to go home."

Aniruddha, realising things had gone too far, understood. It was late, and he offered to drive her home. Ruchika, with no other choice, agreed, though shame and regret weighed heavily on her.

The car ride was silent. Ruchika stared out the window, her mind racing with confusion and guilt. Aniruddha, equally remorseful, respected her silence.

Ruchika had come to Aniruddha hoping to ease her heart, but instead, the night had left her with more emotional weight than she had arrived with. What started as a search for answers ended in unexpected confusion, leaving her unsure of what to do next.

Chapter – XIV

——————※※——————

Months passed, and Ruchika couldn't shake the turmoil in her mind. Instead of worrying about Amit's possible affair, her thoughts turned inward. She felt a growing distance from Amit, as if he were hiding something from her. Even with her unease, Ruchika remained silent, never voicing her concerns or questioning his behaviour.

In her silence, another feeling began to blossom: an attraction to Aniruddha. Their connection from that night lingered, complicating her emotions further. She struggled to understand her feelings, unable to confide in anyone about the shift in her affections. The weight of her unspoken thoughts became an additional burden, leaving her feeling more isolated than ever.

Sometimes, brief phone calls with Aniruddha brought her solace. Their casual conversations provided a welcome distraction, and she found peace in the sound of his voice—a calming presence amid her worries. With each chat, she sensed a bond growing, one that both excited and unsettled her as she navigated her feelings and her situation with Amit.

After that incident, Aniruddha kept his distance from Amit's home, choosing to lay low. He felt the tension from that night linger and believed it was best to step back, missing the camaraderie they once shared. He knew Ruchika needed time to sort through her feelings.

One night, Ruchika was jolted awake by a call from Amit. Surprised to hear his voice at such a late hour, she sensed urgency in his tone. "I need to talk to you about something important," he said, his words slurred. Confused, Ruchika wondered why he chose this moment to reach out.

"Ruchi, I'm so sorry," Amit began, his voice heavy with emotion. "I never wanted to hurt you, but things have spiralled out of control. I've fallen in love with someone else—someone from the office. I can't imagine my life without her."

His words hit Ruchika like a thunderbolt, and her heart sank. "Please leave me," he begged. "I know you're a wonderful wife and mother, but I can't live with you anymore."

As he spoke, Amit touched Ruchika's feet in sorrow, emphasising the weight of his confession. Ruchika stood frozen in shock, grappling with disbelief and heartbreak. Tears welled in her eyes as the reality sank in. With a two-year-old baby, where could she go? How could she leave?

In her mind, a haunting melody began to play, echoing her sorrow: "*Je rate mor duyar guli, bhanglo jhore.*"

("That night, the storm shattered the doors of my heart.")

The lyrics captured her feelings of loss, mirroring the storm within her. Ruchika felt like a statue, trapped in a world of turmoil.

The next morning, desperate for guidance, Ruchika went to Aniruddha's place before his office hours. After Amit's confession, she hadn't slept or focused on her baby. In her urgency, she left her child with a servant and rushed to speak with Aniruddha.

"What brings you here so early, Ruchika? You could have called," Aniruddha said, surprised by her visit.

"I couldn't wait, Aniruddha. Amit asked me to leave him. He's in love with one of your staff members," Ruchika's voice cracked as tears filled her eyes.

"What? How could Amit do this to you? Has he lost his mind?" Aniruddha responded, shocked.

"You knew, didn't you? Why didn't you tell me? How could you hide this from me?" she accused, tears streaming down her face.

"Ruchika, Amit is my friend. I thought he could manage his feelings; after all, he is my friend first, and you come later…" Aniruddha tried to explain.

"Wow, Aniruddha. Now I'm just someone who came after Amit? Have you forgotten that night? How could you forget?" Ruchika shouted, her pain spilling over.

"I've already apologised for that night. We were both drunk. Please don't confuse that with what's happening now," Aniruddha said firmly.

Feeling utterly alone, Ruchika replied, "Fine, Aniruddha. I'm sorry for bothering you," and turned to leave.

Aniruddha stepped out, watching her go. As she reached the door, she looked back and saw him staring at her, filled with helplessness.

"I can't say 'I love you,' Ruchika," Aniruddha called softly. "Because it comes with responsibility. I can't carry that weight with Amit still in the picture. Please, don't come here again. I'm so sorry."

Ruchika left without a word, but his final look haunted her. Every time she closed her eyes, she saw that look—helpless and sorrowful.

The scent of the devil tree stayed with Ruchika, a symbol of everything that had gone wrong. Its dark branches mirrored her tangled emotions. No matter how far she tried to move on, the memory of the tree and what it represented remained rooted in her soul, reminding her of Amit's betrayal and the night that changed everything.

Chapter XV

Ruchika had made it clear to her in-laws that she wanted to pursue her own career. However, her father-in-law firmly opposed the idea, declaring it unacceptable in their home. With a heavy heart, Ruchika decided to leave with her baby, a choice that left her family in shock.

For months, she tried to convince Amit that they shouldn't end their marriage, especially for the sake of their child. But Amit remained resolute, insisting she leave their home as soon as possible. Ruchika spent six agonising months trying everything to salvage their marriage, but ultimately, she resolved to pursue a mutual divorce.

During this tumultuous time, Ruchika endured immense pressure. Her mother desperately tried to change her mind, urging her not to leave her in-laws' home, no matter what Amit had said. Concerned about societal judgement, her mother feared how their relatives would react. Divorce was an unfamiliar concept in their family, and Amit, viewed as a decent man, was well-loved in Ruchika's household. They couldn't understand why she had made this choice.

Ruchika's mother reminded her that marriage was about more than love or co-parenting; it was about standing by one another through every challenge. She insisted that no one could force Ruchika out of her in-laws' home.

But for Ruchika, this wasn't about anyone else's opinions or societal fears. It was about her self-respect. After years of compromise, she could no longer remain in a place where her voice and choices were disregarded.

Some relationships are only meant to last for a certain period. They enter our lives to teach us something, to help us grow, or to guide us through a phase, but not all are meant to endure. Sometimes, they serve their purpose and drift away, leaving behind memories and lessons that shape who we are.

Today, Ruchika left her in-laws' house. She hadn't cried for the past six months, preparing herself to face society alone. She was acutely aware of the responsibilities now resting on her shoulders. In a show of dignity, she chose not to claim alimony from Amit, believing it would only hurt her self-worth.

Ruchika moved into a nearby rented apartment. As she stepped inside, the dam she had built around her emotions broke. She wept as if she had lost someone dear who would never return. Sorrow, pain, and helplessness consumed her, and her cries echoed off the bare walls, the only witnesses to her grief.

Suddenly, she caught the familiar scent of the devil tree wafting in from outside. It was a March evening, and the air carried that distinct fragrance. In that moment, Ruchika clung to the beautiful memories of her past, seeking solace in the comforting aroma. Her tears, mingling with her emotions, seemed to flow away, dissolving into the overwhelming scent of the devil flower, as if the fragrance were absorbing her pain.

She discovered that this profound fragrance held an unbreakable bond with her soul, intertwining itself with every chapter of her life. It wasn't just a scent—it was a silent observer, carrying the essence of her joys, sorrows, and every fleeting moment in between. This aroma, timeless and unwavering, became a keeper of her memories, revisiting her in quiet whispers to remind her of where she had been and who she had become.

As she moved forward, she knew it would remain her faithful companion: a bridge to the past and a gentle guide into the future, enriching her journey with its enduring presence.

The End

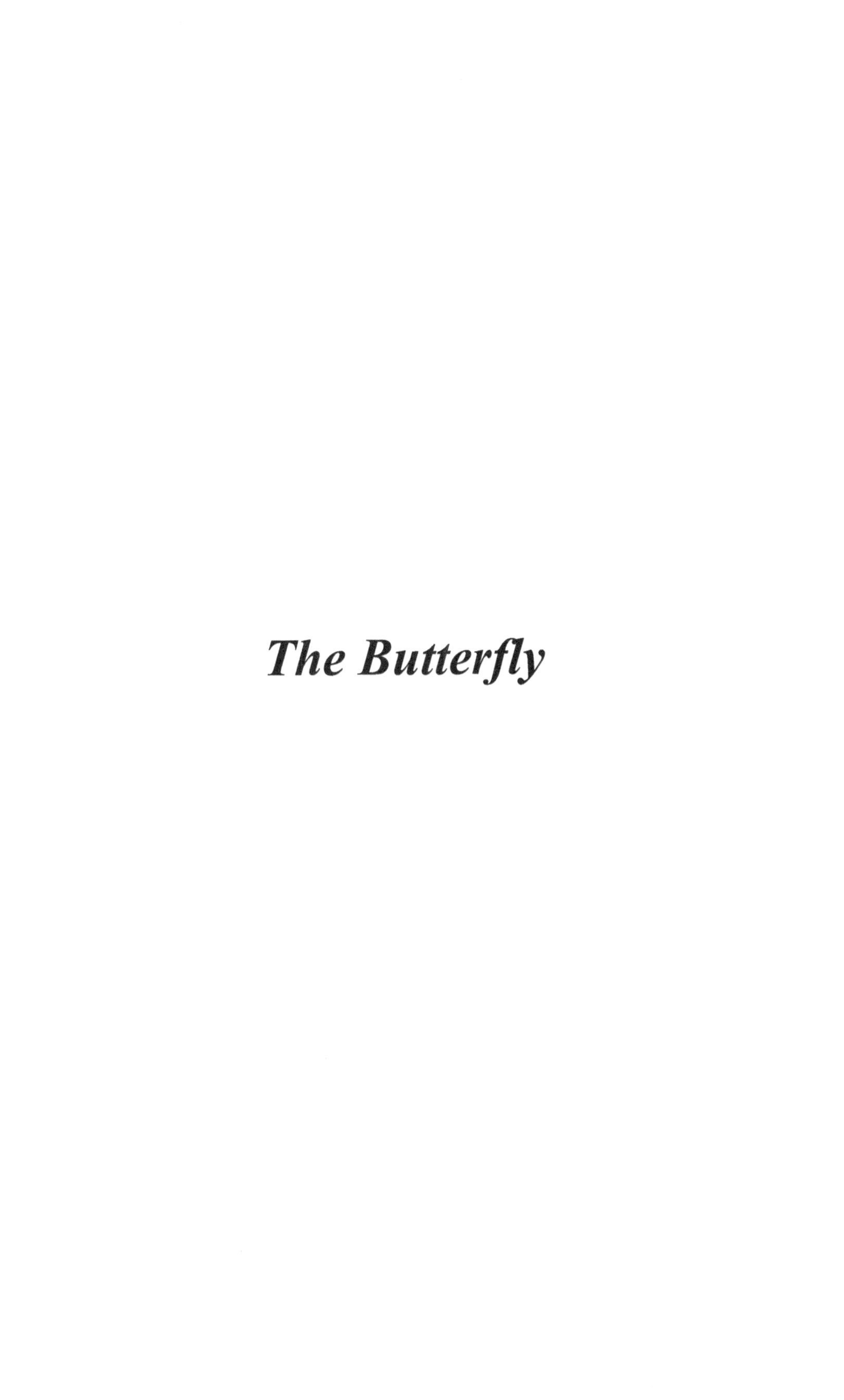

The Butterfly

Chapter I

Dawn in India is a magical time when the world seems to pause, waiting for the new day. The first light appears as a soft blush on the horizon, gently blending night and day. The sky changes from deep blue to lovely shades of pink, orange, and gold as the sun stretches its rays across the land. Birds begin to stir, their soft songs bringing a feeling of peace and hope. The air is cool and fresh, filled with the light scent of wet earth and blooming jasmine, offering a sense of renewal and calm.

In the city, dawn feels like a quiet symphony, where stillness meets the first signs of life. As morning breaks, tall buildings stand like silent guardians against the softening sky. The deep blue of night fades into gentle pinks and oranges, casting a warm glow over the concrete and glass. The busy streets, which were lively just hours before, are now calm, with only a few early risers walking or cycling through the refreshing air.

As the sun climbs higher, the world gradually brightens, filled with a warmth and energy that are special to the Indian dawn. It's a moment for fresh starts, quiet reflection, and truly feeling the heartbeat of life in its simplest form.

I woke up at 3:30 a.m. today. I had already taken leave for the day. Having been raised in metro cities, I'm well aware of almost everything. And being a dynamic career woman, I need to keep myself updated in every aspect.

People hardly get time for any personal space during the weekdays as the city is always running day and night.

Today is a very special day. The first thing I did after freshening up and taking a short bath (since I know I won't have time during the day) was to cook some homemade sweets for my special guest. Guest? Is he a guest? I don't really know.

I got a call at 4:30 a.m., saying that he had arrived at the airport. It will take me hardly 30 minutes to reach the airport this early in the morning. The city is still in a deep sleep.

I catch the cab, and my wristwatch says it's 5:15 a.m., so I'll definitely reach by 5:45 a.m. While in the cab, I'm just recalling everything in my mind—the purpose of rushing to the airport this early morning. Who plans a first date at 6 a.m. in India!

Let me introduce myself first. I'm Meghna Chowdhury, a 35-year-old smart, outspoken, elegant corporate lady. I know my worth. Being a career-oriented woman, my situation hasn't allowed me to get married yet, and I'm happily single by choice. My full focus is on my career, and I can't afford any distractions. I've been living alone in Hyderabad for my job for the last few years. My parents live in a different city. I'm capable enough to take care of myself.

Then suddenly, what's happening to me? The butterflies are flying in my stomach now.

Emotionally, the butterflies in the stomach reflect a powerful connection between mind and body. It's my heart racing with anticipation, my breath quickening, and my thoughts spinning, all captured in that fluttery sensation. It's a beautiful mix of fear and thrill—like standing on the edge of something wonderful, ready to leap into the unknown.

Besides my job, I hardly get time to pursue any hobbies; sometimes, I just play games online to break the monotony. I'm not much of a social media person either.

One day, I suddenly noticed someone kept sending me "lives" when I needed them in my game. I discovered that this person wasn't even in my connections or from any of my friend circles. I'm a little adventurous by nature and love watching thrillers and adventure movies in my free time.

Oh, I should mention that I have a so-called boyfriend, too, whom I only meet on weekends. We've been dating for five years, but there hasn't been any commitment from either side. We're both too busy focusing on our own careers. No romance, no night outs, no hanky-panky, as I've found him to be quite introverted and, frankly, boring.

So, someone is interested in my game, right? Let me connect with him. I selected his name from my game's database and added him to my messenger to send a little "Thank You" message. Was it just a gesture or my inquisitive nature?

Chapter II

"Hi, Meghna here, hope you're doing well. Thank you so much for sending me 'Lives' when I needed them in my game," I said.

Just a few minutes later, I got a reply: "Nice to meet you, Meghna."

This is Raj. Do you know me? And sorry, but I haven't sent any 'Lives' to support you. Actually, I have no idea about any online game."

"Oh, really? But I saw your name and picture there, so I thought I'd say thank you," I responded.

"It doesn't matter. Life is a small circle—you never know whom you'll meet or when. We may not know each other yet, but there's no harm in getting to know one another, right?" he said.

"Yeah, sure, but I hardly get time to chat," I replied.

"Me too, dear. Anyway, you never know—have a great day," he said.

A few days later, I had just finished one of my projects, and with no new ones in sight, plus the directors being out of town, it was the perfect chance to explore the world a little.

"Hey, what's up? How are you?" I messaged Raj.

"All good! How are you, dear? I thought you might not come back," he replied.

"Who told you that? I may not be a social butterfly, but I did check out your profile. I saw you're from Himachal, Shimla, which really caught my attention. I've been there twice, and I absolutely love it! You're lucky—living in heaven!"

"No, dear, I'm actually residing on a ship somewhere in the Middle East," he replied.

"Wow, that's even more interesting! You live on a ship? For how long? Are you talking to me from the ship right now? Is that even possible?" I asked, surprised.

"Why not? It's not a moving ship; it's been stationed in the water for many months. I work for an oil company, and we extract raw oil from the depths of the sea. It's a long process, so the ship stays at the same point for months," he explained.

I felt a sense of adventure rising in me. "Really? I had no idea about this kind of work," I said.

"If you don't mind, I'd love to know more about your profession. Could you share some photos of the ship, please? Hey, do you get to see dolphins swimming around often?" I asked with curiosity.

He sent me laughing emojis and said, "Yeah, I'll send you snaps later, but no, dear, life here isn't so easy. We work 12 hours a day, all 7 days. No holidays, no female faces. After a few days, people start getting irritated."

"Oh, really! I had no idea. I'm really sorry to hear that. I thought it would be more of an adventurous type of job," I replied.

"Adventure for those who are joining newly, and for those sitting in their air-conditioned offices in the city, doing 9-to-6 jobs, looking for short-term thrills in life," he replied, with a hint of arrogance. "Here it's 48 degrees Celsius outside."

I understood he was indirectly pointing at me.

"You're right. It's human nature. We always think everyone else is happier than us because we don't always value what we have. The grass looks greener from a distance," I said.

"So, how did you manage time today for chatting for so long?" he asked.

"Actually, my bosses are going for a trip abroad, and meanwhile, I have submitted my current project, so I get some leisure time to chill," I replied.

"Catch up again with you after lunch, if you are free," I said.

Chapter III

It's the middle of March, and the weather outside is a little pleasant. By the end of this month, my parents are coming to visit me. I need to buy some home items, so I plan to leave the office a little early.

After lunch, I return to my seat, and after completing some official work, I feel the urge to check my chatbot again. It's actually a habit. When you're talking to someone, you slowly get addicted.

I saw two beautiful pictures of the ship in the blue sea, but it's not the kind of ship we usually see. It looks more like a factory with lots of machines, and an orange-dressed person standing in front of it with a smile. He looks like a foreigner with a well-built physique.

Okay, so this is Mr. Raj. Great.

"Hi, are you there?" No reply from the other side.

Anyway, why am I showing so much interest? I'm Meghna Choudhury. I have a steady boyfriend, so to hell with this. Just get lost. Ugh…

After a few hours, I leave the office for the local market nearby, but my mind is occupied elsewhere.

Meghna, don't. This is not a good sign.

The day ends, and Meghna goes to sleep early and wakes up early too. No rush for the office, but still, I need to be punctual. Who knows, something might happen.

Just after entering the office, I got some urgent work, which kept me occupied for another hour. During the tea break, I felt the urge to go online and check if there's anything for me.

"Hi Meghna, good morning. Sorry for the late reply. My shift ends at 2 p.m. India time, so I couldn't reply earlier. I checked your message when I got back from my shift at your midnight," a message from him reads.

Oh, shit! How could I forget? We're in different time zones. He's somewhere in the Middle East, and there's about a 4-hour time difference.

"Good morning! You must be feeling tired after working since midnight," I replied politely.

He's typing something, which means he's online now—great! I feel butterflies running in my stomach.

"Hi Meghna, how are you? I hope you had a good sleep and are at the office now. I'm not feeling tired at all, just a little upset that I haven't seen you since yesterday afternoon," he replied.

"Is that so? Don't you think you're moving too fast?" I said.

"How fast? My ship has been standing here for the last 6 months. How can I go fast? Haha," he typed.

"Okay, Mr. Foreigner, I apologise for making you wait," I replied with a smiley emoji.

"Who's the foreigner? I'm a typical Indian—I love my India," he replied.

"That sounds great. May I know a little more about you?" I asked.

"Sure, why not. I'm a Himachali guy. My father passed away. I have a lovely family—my loving wife, a daughter, a son, my mom, and my grandmother. I work for an American company in the Middle East. I get 28 days of leave after every 2 months. That's the normal schedule," he said.

What?! Is he a married guy?! No, Meghna, no. You can't do this. Are you crazy? You might be single by choice at 35, but most Indians are married by your age. Look at your friends—all married with 1 or 2 kids. Make a move, Meghna; this is not for you. It's your no-go area. Please listen to your brain—don't mess with your heart.

And what did he say? He has a loving wife! No, Meghna, no. Just stop. Keep quiet and walk away.

"Wow, that's nice. You're a lucky guy with a loving family. Great. I hope you or your family wouldn't mind if we became good friends, right?" I wrote.

What is this, Meghna? I warned you—it's your no-go area. Then why? Why are you jumping into a fire? Is it really necessary?

"Yeah, sure, why not. I'd be happy to have you as a friend. Thank you so much," he said.

Chapter IV

Time flows naturally. It moves effortlessly, without haste or stagnation. It's when moments seem to pass in harmony with the rhythm of life, where everything unfolds at its own pace. There's no pressure or urgency—just the gentle, steady progression of events, like the flowing of a river.

We kept chatting almost every day for hours, building an invisible bridge between us. The more we talked, the more addicted we became. We shared our phone numbers along the way, and he started calling me 2-3 times a day, both before and after office hours. Sometimes, even during work.

We began a journey, unknowingly drawing closer. Now, I can't go a single day without him. His voice over the phone drives me crazy. His chat messages mean the world to me. When we weren't talking or chatting, he would send me beautiful emails and letters.

I know I have a boyfriend, and he has a wife, but when I talk to him, I can't think beyond that moment. I forget about all practical and rational things. The dynamic Meghna Chowdhury is now dying for a married man.

In the meantime, my parents visited and left, but I'm now living in a paradise. Nothing touches me. When I walk down the road, I can't see or hear anything—my ears are always filled with his voice. He speaks to me so beautifully, and my mind is constantly full of thoughts of him.

Sometimes, I blush unknowingly. Nothing bothers me, and I feel so happy from deep within my soul.

One day, he asked me what I thought about meeting him when he returns to India, on his way back to Himachal. He said he would take a flight to Hyderabad, with a connecting flight to his hometown, and suggested we meet at the airport during the hours in between his flights.

I found out he would land in India by 4 a.m. and he asked me to meet him at 6 a.m.

At 5:45 a.m., the world outside looked beautiful. The sun hadn't risen yet, and the sky was painted in a yellowish-reddish hue. He was waiting for me outside the airport, and I could see him even from a distance. I felt so shy. I never thought a date could happen at 5:45 in the morning. I felt like I was coming to receive my very special person in life.

The sun would be the witness to our first meeting.

When the sun becomes the witness of a couple's date, it signifies a moment of pure, unspoken beauty. As the first light of dawn breaks, it paints the sky in soft hues of pink, gold, and orange, casting a gentle glow over the world. The quiet serenity of the early morning creates an intimate atmosphere, as if nature itself is pausing to honour the moment.

In this peaceful setting, the couple stands together, their hearts connected, sharing something so personal that even the rising sun feels like a silent companion. The warmth of the sunlight, not yet harsh, wraps them in a golden embrace, making the moment feel eternal, as if time itself has slowed down just for them. The entire world is still, and in that brief span, they feel as though they are the only two people alive, with the sun as their quiet, radiant witness to a love that transcends words.

I had a rough idea that his connecting flight would be in another 5-6 hours, so we could spend some time over a coffee and a break first in a nearby area. Though I know nothing is going to open before 8 am. But after meeting him, I came to know that his next flight is in the evening at 7 pm, and he has already booked a hotel in the airport area, so now we are going there.

I was not prepared for this surprise as it's a very unethical proposal for Meghna Chowdhury.

Anyway, we are going to the hotel and spent almost a whole day with Raj Mahera.

I get to know many more things about him. We are just totally fascinated with each other. Things may go wrong, but we are just going beyond all right and wrong.

Love is blind to flaws and free from judgement. It goes beyond all limits, seeing only the heart's true essence. When I look at him, I can't help but feel he embodies everything that makes a great partner. He is endlessly caring, always watching over me with a protective warmth that makes me feel safe and valued. His manners are impeccable, combining grace and thoughtfulness, making it hard to resist his presence. He possesses a quiet strength and kindness that makes me want him by my side for a lifetime.

When someone looks you in the eye and honestly says he loves his wife but has also fallen for you, who am I to judge? Love is complex and unpredictable, often defying reason. It doesn't fit neatly into boxes or follow rules. I have no right to judge his feelings because love isn't always something we can control; it simply happens.

Love knows no boundaries; it flows freely, untouched by time, distance, or circumstances. Even if I move away from him physically, the deeper connection—the bond in my soul—remains. It's not just about being close; it's about the connection that has woven itself into my being. Leaving him may be possible, but letting go of that soulful bond feels much harder, maybe even impossible.

When people love deeply, they see beyond differences and barriers. It doesn't matter if they are separated by miles, cultures, or life situations. Love can bridge gaps that seem impossible to cross, uniting hearts in a way that defies logic or expectation.

This reflects love's limitless nature; it doesn't follow rules, obey schedules, or conform to what society expects. It simply exists, powerful and enduring, embracing the freedom to be shared without boundaries.

There are countless reasons why Meghana is falling in love with Raj—his kindness, his warmth, his understanding, and the little gestures that draw her closer. However, there's one undeniable reason holding her back: he's a married man. That single truth casts a shadow over everything, making it hard for her to fully accept his love, no matter how strong the attraction.

We shared a kiss, an intimate moment so deep and intense that it felt like the outside world faded away. In that sacred space, we made a vow to each other—to be together, no matter what. We promised to do whatever it takes to make it happen, but with one important condition: we would never hurt our partners. We would navigate this delicate situation with care, honouring both our love and the lives we are already part of.

Chapter V

In the time between our next meeting, we found ourselves falling even deeper for each other, feeling it was time to take our relationship to the next level. While he couldn't pursue another legal marriage, we were both drawn to the idea of sealing our bond in a way that transcended formalities. Together, we decided on a "Gandharva" marriage—a spiritual and eternal union that didn't require legal recognition but held deep meaning for us.

I've already begun preparing for our special day. He shared his next visit to India, and this time, he will come directly to my apartment, where we will marry. I've bought two rings for us, symbols of the commitment we'll exchange, and I've also purchased "*sindoor*" from a nearby temple to mark the sacred moment. I've made plans to decorate my entire home with flowers, getting ready for not just our wedding but also our "*Suhagraat.*" Though he'll arrive early in the morning, we'll carry out the customs together as daylight breaks, creating an intimate ceremony just for us.

Though I feel a pang of guilt about my boyfriend, I've realised that what we share isn't truly love—it's more of a habit, a comfortable familiarity. As hard as it is to admit, I've had to acknowledge that our bond lacks the depth I've now found elsewhere. I know I'll have to be honest with him about my new relationship soon. I owe him that truth, even though it won't be easy.

Meghna Chowdhury, 35, and Raj Malhotra, 40—two mature individuals—made the bold choice to bind themselves together for life, without considering the possible consequences of their decision. Despite their age and life experience, this spontaneous act of love and commitment may reveal itself to be impulsive and immature, bringing unforeseen challenges in the future. Yet, in that moment, they chose to follow their hearts, leaving the uncertainties for later.

The day finally arrived, and Meghna and Raj created the beautiful moments they had envisioned together. In that atmosphere of love and celebration, Meghna felt a deep sense of completeness, experiencing the affection she had long sought for many years. The best part about Raj was his natural ability to bring joy to her life; he truly understood how to make her happy. For the first time in his life, even after being married for over twelve years, Raj found himself surrounded by the passion and warmth that Meghna radiated, deepening their connection in a way he had never experienced before. Their union was not just a ceremony; it was a celebration of love, fulfilment, and newfound joy.

After their marriage, Meghna felt a surge of enthusiasm and a strong desire to invest in their relationship. As an independent and intelligent woman, she was eager to embrace life as a normal couple would, revelling in this new experience. Excitedly, she began planning a honeymoon for the two of them, imagining romantic adventures and cherished memories they would create together.

In her excitement, Meghna forgot the real situation they were in. She temporarily overlooked that Raj was still a married man with two children depending on him. While she wanted to celebrate their love, the complications in their lives faded from her mind, leaving her happily focused on their union.

Raj started to feel awkward as Meghna talked about wanting a honeymoon and a normal relationship. He knew her wishes were normal and that she deserved happiness, but as a married man, he struggled with the ethical issues of their relationship. He felt torn between his love for Meghna and his responsibilities to his wife and children. This internal conflict made it hard for him to manage his feelings and obligations.

Both Meghna and Raj felt a lot of mental pressure as they faced the hard truths of their situation. For Meghna, it was tough. Even though she was smart and mature enough to understand the reality, it didn't make things easier. She felt sad about having to step back, even though she didn't want to.

Deep down, she just wanted to create happiness for both of them. However, she realised that true happiness couldn't exist if one of them wasn't fully on board. This understanding weighed heavily on her, forcing her to think about the complexities of their relationship and the sacrifices needed to respect everyone involved.

Out of love, Raj wanted to make Meghna happy. Understanding her desires, he decided to surprise her with a honeymoon plan in Kashmir. He pushed aside all the worries and focused on how happy this would make her. He paid attention to every detail, hoping to create a magical experience that would help them enjoy their connection, even if just for a short time, amid their complicated lives. In this choice, he wanted to bring a little happiness to both of their hearts.

Raj planned a surprise three-day honeymoon for Meghna, creating a memorable experience filled with joy and intimacy. As they enjoyed the stunning beauty of Kashmir, they laughed, shared secrets, and cherished every moment together. Each sunrise and sunset became part of their best memories, filled with warmth and connection. Those days became a special part of their hearts, promising to be remembered for a lifetime—a beautiful escape that allowed them to savour their love despite their complicated lives.

If "honeymoon" means a time for relaxation, exploration, and building a deeper emotional connection, then that's exactly what they had. It was an intimate getaway focusing on their unique love story and the journey they were starting together. He did everything he could to make that trip unforgettable for both of them.

After their heartfelt marriage and beautiful honeymoon, Meghna was filled with hope and excitement for what life could bring them. Naturally, she wanted more—more shared moments, more adventures, and a deeper connection with Raj. She began to express her desire for quality time together, eager to nurture the bond they had created. Every moment spent with him deepened her affection and made her long for a future filled with love and companionship, as she dreamed of building a life that reflected the joy they had experienced together.

However, Raj started to struggle with meeting Meghna's expectations. With nearly eight months spent on his demanding job, often travelling abroad, he found it hard to find the time he wanted to dedicate to her. After all that time, he only had four months to spend with his family, and Meghna's increasing pressure for more quality time added to his stress.

Despite his love for Meghna, Raj felt caught between his responsibilities and the desire to meet her needs. This tension grew as he tried to balance the demands of his family and his relationship with Meghna. Each day became a reminder of the limitations he faced, complicating the once beautiful connection they had shared.

Chapter VI

Just after returning from their honeymoon, Meghna was given a new project and became the team leader. Suddenly, she was overwhelmed with responsibilities at work. Her days stretched to nearly 10 hours, leaving her completely exhausted when she got home, as if the weight of the day had drained her entirely.

Meanwhile, Raj returned to his ship right after the honeymoon, this time departing directly from Hyderabad. He wouldn't be back for another two months. Meghna found it challenging to stay in touch, as her busy schedule barely allowed for even brief chats. They were both learning to adjust to their new realities. Raj still made time to call her twice a day, but their conversations had become more formal, filled with routine exchanges. During one of these calls, Meghna learned that Raj wouldn't be able to visit her next time. Due to urgent family matters in Himachal, he would take a direct flight there and only plan to meet her on his way back to the ship.

This meant that Meghna would have to wait a full three months before seeing Raj again. This realisation left her feeling slightly unsettled, but she knew there wasn't much she could do. Life had been moving at a relentless pace, and she had barely kept up with her usual routine, including her health check-ups. One evening, arriving home a bit earlier than usual, she found herself missing Raj deeply. Two months had already passed since he left, and she knew he was now at his family home. As she thought about him, a sudden question struck her—had she missed her period this time? She couldn't quite remember. Had she missed it last month as well? This was unusual for her. Meghna had always been vigilant about such matters, but with her workload and the whirlwind of responsibilities after the honeymoon, she hadn't noticed.

Adding to her anxiety was the fact that her boyfriend had visited her 5 or 6 times in the past two months. Now, Meghna felt a rising sense of panic, a feeling of being trapped. Despite being a modern, self-assured woman, this change in her cycle created enormous mental pressure. She knew she needed to talk to Raj first, remembering how carefree they had been during their honeymoon, caught up in their emotions. Her boyfriend, on the other hand, was always very cautious and never careless about such matters. Still, there was a chance that something could have gone wrong.

The first thing Meghna needed to do was check herself, but she felt it was necessary to inform Raj about this unusual situation first. As the clock ticked towards 10 o'clock at night, sweat began to gather on her brow. She needed to calm down. Taking a deep breath, she dialled Raj's number. Two possibilities flashed through her mind—either Raj would answer and understand immediately that this was an emergency, or his wife might pick up the phone. Preparing herself for the latter, Meghna steeled herself for the conversation that could unfold.

As the phone rang, Meghna's heart raced, but no one picked up. She had prepared herself for the possibility that another woman might answer, ready with a quick excuse if needed. When the call went unanswered, she figured Raj would surely call her back during his morning walk, as he often did when he was home. The anticipation lingered, and she clung to the hope that he would reach out and close the gap that felt ever-widening between them.

As she had anticipated, Raj called Meghna early the next morning during his walk, but the conversation quickly turned into an argument. He questioned her about why she had called so late, knowing he couldn't answer. Meghna was taken aback, realising how heartless he seemed in that moment, focused only on his own situation and not on her feelings.

Raj explained that his wife had seen the call and asked him who had called so late at night. He struggled to convince her that it could have been an emergency, but his wife insisted he call the number back in front of her. Although he had saved Meghna's contact under a different name to protect her privacy, this made things even more complicated for him.

Meghna felt as though she had been slapped in the face instead of receiving the understanding and affection she had hoped for when she reached out. In that moment, the warmth she craved felt distant, replaced by the weight of Raj's frustration and the realisation that her actions had inadvertently caused trouble for him.

Meghna couldn't bring herself to share the mental and physical strain she was under. She felt no need to explain why she had called Raj the previous night. Her self-respect held her back, refusing to let her speak beyond what her dignity allowed. Despite the whirlwind of emotions and uncertainty swirling within her, she made a firm decision: she would never let Raj know what was happening to her. Some things, she resolved, were better kept to herself, even if they weighed heavily on her soul.

In truth, both Meghna and Raj were valid in their feelings and concerns about their situation. Their love for each other ran deep, filled with passion and connection. However, the only thing standing in their way was "the time." Life's demands and responsibilities were pulling them in different directions, making it hard for them to fully embrace their love. If only they could align their circumstances with their hearts, they might find a way to navigate the complexities of their relationship.

Meghna struggled to express why she felt like an "option" rather than a "priority."

Chapter VII

Meghna had made up her mind—she would never bow her head before anyone. Love would not weaken her. Whatever challenges life threw her way, she was determined to face them head-on, alone if necessary.

By 7 a.m., Meghna picked up the phone and scheduled an appointment with a gynaecologist. She decided to visit the doctor before heading to the office. Today, she was up and ready earlier than usual, preparing herself mentally for whatever lay ahead. At 8 a.m., she discreetly arrived at the hospital. After a quick preliminary checkup, the doctor delivered the news that hit her like a bolt of lightning—Meghna was pregnant. It felt as if the ground had slipped from beneath her feet. The doctor, unaware of her inner turmoil, congratulated her and recommended further tests—blood work, urine samples, and an ultrasound—to confirm the pregnancy with certainty.

Meghna, still in shock, explained to the doctor that she wasn't sure how many menstrual cycles she had missed due to her overwhelming work schedule.

With the tests done, she made her way to the office, feeling numb but resolved to stay composed. The results would be ready by the evening, and she promised herself that once she had them in hand, she would figure out her next steps. Until then, she had to hold herself together and keep moving forward.

Meghna already understood the gravity of the situation—what a blunder she had made. The uncertainty gnawed at her, and she couldn't even be sure whose baby this was. Though a part of her held onto the hope that it might be Raj's, the uncertainty clouded her thoughts. She knew she couldn't share this news with her family; not a single word could slip to her colleagues or friends either.

She felt utterly alone, carrying the weight of this secret as she anxiously waited for the evening to arrive, knowing that the answers she sought—and the decisions she would have to make—were just hours away.

After reaching the office, Meghna quickly got absorbed in her usual work routine. Since she had arrived a little late, the workload felt heavier than usual. As the afternoon wore on, she received an unexpected call from Raj. His voice carried a tone of apology for his behaviour that morning. Raj, always attentive, had sensed something was off in Meghna's demeanour. He expressed concern, hinting that he could feel something was troubling her.

But Meghna remained silent. She couldn't bring herself to say a word, not now, not with so much uncertainty swirling inside her. Raj's voice continued on the other end, but she found herself lost in her own thoughts, holding back the storm of emotions that threatened to spill out.

The very next day, Meghna returned to the hospital, having already applied for a 2-3 days leave. After reviewing all her reports, the doctor confirmed that Meghna was indeed pregnant—two months along, to be exact. The ultrasound showed that the baby was developing perfectly. However, her blood work revealed some deficiencies; she was low in iron and had a concerning haemoglobin level. The doctor prescribed the necessary supplements and strongly advised her to rest for a few days, as it was the very early stage of her pregnancy. Additionally, she recommended Meghna return for her next visit with the baby's father.

At this moment, Meghna realised she needed to speak up. Gathering her thoughts, she told the doctor that she didn't want to keep the baby, explaining that she wasn't married yet.

The doctor, surprised and a bit taken aback, gently but firmly scolded Meghna for considering such a decision. She urged her to think carefully, pointing out that Meghna was already 35 and should involve her boyfriend in the conversation before making any irreversible choices. The doctor emphasised the importance of taking responsibility for both their relationship and the baby, and advised Meghna to reconsider the gravity of her decision.

Meghna knew exactly what needed to be done. She mustered the courage and called her boyfriend, informing him about the situation and asking for his help. Although she hadn't expected much—certainly not for him to react with sympathy—his response surprised her. Without hesitation, he took responsibility for the situation and rushed to meet her at the hospital, arriving within the hour.

This unexpected show of support from him gave Meghna a momentary sense of relief. The weight of uncertainty she had been carrying alone for days now felt a little lighter, knowing she wasn't entirely alone in facing what lay ahead.

He didn't ask a single question, offering Meghna unwavering support in every way possible to help her navigate this difficult and unexpected situation. By evening, everything was resolved, and Meghna returned to her apartment in the comforting presence of her boyfriend, who gently carried her inside. She felt a deep sense of relief, knowing that she could finally rest.

Exhausted, Meghna extended her leave from work, sending an email to request an additional 2-3 days off, citing unavoidable circumstances. Now, in the quiet of her apartment, she could focus on recovering, both physically and emotionally, with a renewed sense of clarity.

As soon as her boyfriend left, Meghna broke down, her emotions flooding in all at once. Tears streamed down her face as she grappled with the overwhelming sorrow of what had just happened. If her life had been more stable, if she had the normal, loving conjugal life she had always dreamed of *this baby* would have been the happiest moment of her life. Meghna had always loved children, and the thought of becoming a mother had once filled her with joy.

But now, the reality was too painful to bear. She had never imagined that one day she would have to make such a heart-wrenching decision—ending the life of her own child before it even had a chance to live. The guilt and grief consumed her, and as she sat alone in her apartment, her sobs echoed through the quiet, a haunting reminder of the life that could have been.

The most beautiful moment for any woman is often the chance to become a mother, and Meghna felt that opportunity slip through her fingers. The weight of her decision settled heavily on her heart, and the guilt was suffocating. Each day, it would be a struggle—reminders of what could have been would haunt her, gnawing at her soul.

Every time she saw a mother with her child, every laugh of a happy baby, or even the mention of pregnancy would serve as a painful reminder of the life she had chosen to end. This guilt threatened to consume her, turning into a relentless shadow that followed her wherever she went, leaving her to question her choices and the path her life had taken. The ache of longing and regret would be her constant companion, a reminder of the joy she had always dreamed of but now felt forever out of reach.

Chapter VIII

For the next two days, Meghna didn't receive any calls from Raj. He remained unaware of the turmoil that had unfolded in her life, leaving her alone with her thoughts and the weight of her decision. In her heart, Meghna made an oath to herself that she would never reveal this truth to Raj. It was a secret she intended to carry alone, no matter how heavy it felt.

Eventually, life began to settle back into its normal routine, resuming its course as if nothing had changed. Meghna immersed herself in work, throwing herself into her tasks to distract from the pain that lingered beneath the surface. Yet, the echoes of her past decisions would always remain, a quiet reminder of the life she had chosen, even as the world around her moved on.

Life truly is the best teacher, imparting lessons through a tapestry of experiences, both good and bad. Each moment serves as a valuable lesson, shaping who we are and guiding us along our journey. The joys teach us gratitude and appreciation, while the hardships cultivate resilience and strength. Through every challenge and triumph, we learn to navigate the complexities of existence, emerging wiser and more compassionate. Ultimately, it's these experiences that enrich our lives, deepening our understanding of ourselves and the world around us.

No one could see the old, cheerful Meghna anymore; she had changed profoundly. Each day at the office, she went through the motions—completing her tasks, hardly engaging with her colleagues, and returning home in silence. When Raj called, expressing his apologies more than a hundred times for his earlier rudeness, Meghna felt a distance that had never been there before. The affection that once flowed so freely between them had waned, replaced by an unshakeable emptiness. Something essential was missing.

Raj was unaware of the loss that had fundamentally altered Meghna's life. He couldn't fathom the depth of her pain or the weight of her secret, and his apologies felt inadequate against the backdrop of her sorrow. Meghna was dying inside, each day a struggle to mask the grief that lingered just beneath her composed exterior. The laughter and light she once carried had dimmed, leaving her to navigate a world that felt increasingly isolating and hollow. Each passing moment became a reminder of the life she could have had, and with each breath, the ache of her choices grew heavier.

Almost two years have passed.

They hardly meet each other—only when he goes back home, which means once every two months, and only for 2-3 hours.

Megna found herself comparing two people in her life. One, who never complained or made excuses, came to meet her every week—even during emergencies—yet rarely expressed his feelings. The other, who barely found time to see her and was never there during her moments of need, constantly expressed his emotions about her. Was Megna fooling herself? Was she playing with her own emotions?

Megna is an intelligent woman, but she can no longer endure the emotional turmoil. She's practical and spends most of her time focused on her job. On the other hand, she knew that Raj's wife, a housewife with little formal education, kept herself busy caring for their home and children. She is sincere, dedicated, and loves Raj deeply, waiting patiently for him month after month. Megna even felt sympathy for her. She never intended to break up a family—whatever she did was driven purely by the love and affection that had been missing from her life, even while being in a long-term relationship.

One more thing Meghna has noticed is that he comes for her 12-14 days a year. Most of the time, he's on the ship, and during that time, they are 100% connected. But once he goes back home for 28 days, he isn't able to talk to her. That haunts Meghna a lot, especially at night. After a whole day of working, when she is lying in bed, knowing that he is now sleeping with his legal wife, she just can't accept that.

Day by day, she started to realise that this relationship is actually very impractical. It was not a good decision for her at all. He loves his family and his wife a lot. Whenever he bought something for Meghna, he always bought it in pairs—one for her and one for his wife. When they went out, she noticed that he talked to his wife five times a day. And she felt guilt in my mind. As a woman, knowing everything from the very first day, she felt like she was cheating another woman. She still felt guilty for him as well. She saw how divided he was, trying to give her justice. It was incredibly difficult for him.

One day, seemingly out of nowhere, Raj became overwhelmed with emotion and broke down in tears. Through his sobs, he confessed that he didn't feel like he was a good husband or even a good lover. Speaking from a place of deep guilt, he admitted that he had doubts about whether he should have ever entered Megna's life, feeling that he wasn't the right person for her and that she deserved someone better.

When a man cries because of love, helplessness, and guilt, it shows that he is feeling very vulnerable and has a mix of complicated emotions that he might struggle to put into words. Here's a simpler breakdown of these feelings:

1. **Crying out of Love**: Tears from love come from strong feelings of affection and connection to someone. When a man loves deeply, he might cry because that love feels so powerful. This kind of crying shows how much the person or relationship means to him.

2. **Crying out of Helplessness**: When a man feels helpless, it means he thinks he can't change a situation or make things better, especially in a relationship. This feeling can come from not being able to meet his partner's needs or fix problems. Crying here is often due to frustration and feeling like he has no control over what is happening.

3. **Crying out of Guilt**: Tears of guilt happen when he feels really sorry for something he did or didn't do that hurt the other person. He might feel like he has let his partner down or not met expectations, leading to strong feelings of guilt that make him cry.

When these emotions come together, it creates a strong emotional release. Crying shows that he cares a lot but also feels weighed down by his mistakes or inability to fix things. It's a powerful expression of love mixed with pain, showing the complex struggle he feels inside.

When Meghna entered this relationship, knowing everything from the very beginning, she had no idea how painful it would be to share her man with another woman. It's beyond any explanation. Love happens, but it's difficult to maintain a relationship in this way.

Meghna realised deep in her heart that Raj was a genuine person, and there was no question about his humanity and morality. However, she understood that when someone falls deeply in love, it becomes difficult to balance overwhelming emotions with the weight of responsibility. Love, in its purest form, can blur the lines between emotional vulnerability and rational decision-making, making it challenging to manage both personal feelings and the practical duties that come with a relationship.

Pain in an extramarital affair often comes from the emotional complexities, guilt, and conflicting loyalties involved. Although an affair might bring moments of passion or excitement, it is usually surrounded by deep emotional turmoil. Here's a simpler breakdown of the sources of pain in such situations:

1. **Guilt and Shame**: A major source of pain is the guilt that arises from betraying a spouse or partner. The person having the affair often feels dishonest and ashamed, knowing they are hurting someone they promised to love and protect.

2. **Fear of Exposure**: The constant worry about being discovered can cause a lot of anxiety. Living a double life means keeping secrets, and the pressure to hide everything can be overwhelming, making it hard to find peace of mind.

3. **Emotional Conflict**: People in affairs often develop strong emotional ties to both their spouse and the person they are involved with. This conflict can create confusion and emotional

exhaustion, leaving them feeling torn between two relationships and unable to fully commit to either.

4. **Temporary Fulfilment, Long-term Consequences**: While an affair might offer short-term excitement or satisfaction, it usually leads to long-term problems, like loss of trust, broken families, and damage to personal integrity.

5. **Uncertainty and Instability**: Affairs often lack a stable foundation because they are secretive and uncertain. This instability can create emotional turmoil, leaving the person unsure about the future and whether the relationship can survive if exposed.

Chapter IX

After two years together, Raj planned a vacation for both of them for seven days. He thought they needed more time to reconnect since he hadn't been able to spend enough time with her, and their relationship had been getting worse. But what he hoped would bring them closer ended up being a difficult decision. After spending those seven days together, Meghna realised how much she had misjudged the situation.

One afternoon, Meghna waited in the hotel while Raj went out to take care of some work. He asked her to be ready later for a sightseeing trip. Raj came back around lunchtime, and they had lunch together at a nearby restaurant. After lunch, they explored the local markets because Raj wanted to buy gifts for his family. He picked out dresses for his daughter and wife and encouraged Meghna to choose something for herself. However, Meghna wasn't interested in shopping. She didn't feel right buying things for herself with Raj's money. She was okay with receiving gifts but didn't want to pick something out herself.

Next, they went to a jewellery market, where Raj bought a lovely gold necklace for his daughter. Once again, he urged Meghna to choose something for herself. But she felt uncomfortable with the idea and declined. Accepting gifts was fine, but asking for something made her uneasy.

Later, they visited a nearby beach and sat quietly for hours, watching the sun set. Even though it was a beautiful scene, Meghna felt restless. Something was bothering her, but she couldn't figure out what it was. Although Raj had been with her for the past several days, she felt they weren't truly connected anymore, like they had been during their honeymoon.

This realisation weighed heavily on her. She understood that spending time together hadn't healed the emotional distance between them. The closeness they once had felt out of reach, leaving her feeling lost and disconnected.

Meghna knew she couldn't blame anyone else for how things had turned out. Deep down, she recognised that she often avoided challenges in her relationships. This was a major reason why she had never wanted a traditional marriage. She tended to stay away from situations that required her to deal with complicated emotions, preferring to keep a safe distance from anything that was too emotionally demanding.

It wasn't that she didn't care; it was just that dealing with difficult emotions was overwhelming for her. This habit of stepping back instead of facing issues directly had become a pattern in her life. At moments like these, she saw how much this habit had affected her relationships. The weight of her avoidance felt heavier than ever, and she realised that this pattern needed to change if she wanted to improve her connection with Raj.

They returned to the hotel that night around dinnertime. After eating, Raj wanted to be intimate, but Meghna didn't feel inclined.

Without saying a word, he turned away and fell into a deep sleep, leaving her feeling distant and alone. Meghna struggled to find rest for half the night before finally drifting off.

When she woke up in the morning, Raj was already dressed and ready to leave. He was in town for training for seven days, and this trip had been meant to bring them closer. They had breakfast together, but Raj didn't mention anything about her late start or ask if she had slept well. The silence hung between them, amplifying Meghna's feelings of loneliness. Their conversation felt formal and distant, and soon Raj was off again, leaving her alone in the hotel.

With the entire day stretching before her, Meghna felt a profound sense of weakness from her restless night and the swirling thoughts in her mind. As the hours passed, she reflected deeply on her situation. Finally, she made a decision: she would quit this unhealthy, uncomfortable relationship. It was clear to her that the emotional disconnect had taken a toll on her well-being, and it was time to prioritise her own happiness and peace of mind.

When love and affection start to fade between two people because of pressure and responsibilities, it can be very discouraging. Here's how this often happens:

1. Emotional Distance: The warmth and closeness that once filled the relationship can turn into feelings of coldness and distance. Conversations become shallow, and shared moments feel forced, leading to a sense of being alone.

2. Resentment and Frustration: As responsibilities increase, people may start to feel overwhelmed. This pressure can lead to resentment, both towards themselves for not meeting

expectations and towards their partner for adding to the stress. Frustration can build when one feels unappreciated or unsupported.

3. Loss of Connection: The joyful moments that used to bring the couple together may fade away. Daily routines and obligations take the place of fun and spontaneity, creating a lack of shared experiences that help strengthen their bond. This loss of connection can feel like losing a part of oneself.

4. Doubt and Insecurity: When love begins to fade, people might start to question if the relationship can survive. They may wonder if they are still a good match or if their partner truly understands them. This doubt can cause insecurity, leading to overthinking and anxiety.

5. Longing for the Past: Memories of happier times can become bittersweet. People may find themselves thinking back to when things were easier and more joyful, which can make them feel even more sad about what they've lost.

6. Emotional Exhaustion: Constantly dealing with life's pressures while feeling disconnected from a partner can be very tiring. The effort to keep the relationship going may start to feel like a heavy load instead of a source of happiness, leading to exhaustion and a desire to pull away.

7. Yearning for Fulfilment: There may be a strong desire for emotional satisfaction that feels harder to reach. People might crave a deeper connection that feels meaningful, but it seems increasingly out of reach as love fades.

In essence, when love and affection die under the weight of pressure and responsibility, it can create a profound sense of grief, as both individuals mourn not just the relationship, but also the emotional connection and support they once shared. It's a painful experience that often prompts reflection and the need for change, whether that means working to revive the relationship or ultimately deciding to part ways for the sake of personal well-being.

Chapter X

After a long day spent alone in the hotel, Meghna had finally made her decision. She felt an unexpected calm settle within her; it seemed that the turmoil of indecision had been far more distressing than the act of speaking out about her emotions. When Raj arrived at his usual time, he asked her if she wanted to visit some nearby places. Instead of feeling anxious, Meghna felt a sense of tranquillity.

"Let's sit for a moment," she suggested, knowing this could very well be their last outing together. Raj, sensing her need for connection, offered to order drinks and snacks, hoping to share some intimate moments. Meghna agreed, fully aware that a few drinks might help loosen the tight grip of her emotions.

As they settled in, she realised she was ready to carry their relationship forward, even if she didn't fully grasp the pain, it could bring in the future. Meghna had already paid dearly for her impulsive decisions, and while she couldn't place blame on anyone else, the regret of never becoming a mother lingered heavily in her heart.

In that moment, she knew she had to speak her truth, to unburden herself of the weight she had been carrying. With each sip of her drink, she steeled herself, ready to confront the emotions that had held her captive for too long.

After drinking two large glasses of vodka, Meghna finally found the courage to speak. "Do you really want to know, Raj, what happened that night?" she asked, her voice shaking.

Raj looked confused. "Which night?" he replied, surprised.

Tears streamed down Meghna's face as she continued. "What happened to us? We lost our baby, Raj! We lost our baby…" Her voice broke as she sobbed, grabbing at his chest in pain.

Raj froze, feeling like a statue as her words hit him hard. He felt confused, and then a heavy guilt washed over him. "What are you saying? When did this happen?" he stammered, trying to understand the seriousness of her words.

Meghna's despair grew; she started banging her head against the wall, crying out, "I'm a killer! I killed my own baby! God will never forgive me! Why didn't you take my call that night? Why do you always think only of yourself? I needed you too, Raj! I needed you badly!"

Raj was speechless, unable to find the words. He sat there, shocked by what Meghna had just revealed. He felt the weight of her loss, realising the deep pain of a mother mourning the child she would never hold. It was a burden he never wanted to put on her, but now they were trapped in their grief and guilt.

They had a flight home the next morning, but neither Meghna nor Raj could sleep. The heaviness of their conversation lingered in the air, a painful reminder of their shared sorrow.

Meghna lay awake, her mind racing with emotions. The tears had stopped, but the sadness remained, wrapping around her like a thick fog. She kept replaying the night's revelations in her mind, feeling the weight of her loss and regret. Facing a life filled with grief and unresolved feelings felt too much to handle.

Meanwhile, Raj stared at the ceiling, guilt eating away at him. He felt helpless, realising he had been unaware of Meghna's suffering. Every apology he had given seemed too small for her pain. He knew he needed to do better, but the enormity of her loss felt overwhelming, and he didn't know how to comfort her.

As the hours passed, they each struggled with their thoughts in silence. The darkness of the night made their feelings even stronger. The upcoming flight felt like a turning point, but they were stuck in a moment that required deep reflection. With dawn approaching, they understood that whatever was next would force them to face not just their grief but also the future of their relationship.

Chapter XI

They reached Hyderabad airport by 9:30 am in the morning. Raj wasn't feeling well, so he went to the medical shop inside the airport to get some medicine. Raj requested me to go back home and take rest, as it had been a hectic trip for us, both physically and emotionally. I refused to leave early. His connecting flight to return to his hometown was after 4 hours.

Meghna Chowdhury was waiting alone inside the airport, gathering her thoughts on how to tell Raj that she was going to end this "beautiful mess" of her life. It was hard, but she had to clear things now.

Meghna's so-called boyfriend had already got a hint when she went on this vacation trip. Though he didn't say anything, he had guessed everything. After 2 years of this unethical relationship, Meghna now understood what was more important to her in life.

Raj came back after some time with medicine, water, and coffee for Meghna.

"Raj, what we've had together for the last 2 years, it's been beautiful. It was a wonderful journey for me. But I don't want to walk more steps with you in this journey. I feel that if we continue, the beauty of our relationship will be ruined, and I never want to experience that. I want to keep this journey as a sweet memory for a lifetime. I respect your family, and I value your emotions. We can talk sometimes, for sure, but I don't want to meet you again in the future. This is our last meeting. Thank you so much for everything you've given me up until now, and my best wishes will always be with you as a well-wisher," Meghna said.

Raj didn't say anything, just asked Meghna to take a cab and go home.

****

Now, 15 years later, Meghna has changed her job and received promotions in her new company. She wears glasses now, and most of her hair has turned grey, though she still colours it. She is no longer in contact with her boyfriend. Her father passed away a few years ago, and her mother is living with her now. All the memories have become faded over time.

Some days, Meghna still finds tears in her eyes. She never married again, as she feels emotionally tied to Raj. Some nights, she feels very "blue."

Sometimes, she receives calls from Raj, but they are just brief and formal. She learns that his daughter has gotten married and is now settled in the USA. His son has completed his degree in computer science and is still working at the same job. Raj never asks Meghna to meet him again.

Meghna lies in the darkness, feeling the weight of her thoughts. She can't help but wonder what her life would have been like if things had turned out differently. If she had become a mother, that baby would be 15 years old now, on the brink of becoming a teenager, full of dreams and hopes.

With a deep breath, she imagines those possibilities: the laughter of a child, the milestones, and the small joys of motherhood. It is a bittersweet daydream, filled with warmth and longing, but also a sharp sense of loss. The idea of guiding a teenager through life and sharing in their successes and challenges feels like a glimpse into another world—one where her dreams had come true instead of fading away.

In that moment, Meghna takes a deep breath, trying to focus on reality. She knows she has to move forward, even if the path is painful. The life she imagined is no longer hers, but the memories of what could have been still haunt her. As the first light of dawn starts to shine through the window, she resolves to find a way to honour that lost dream while also embracing the future, whatever it may bring.

One sudden day Megna checked her old email messages and got some old letters from Raj…

The first letter from Raj.

My Dear Loving Meghna,

It's been so many days now since we have been together, but still, it's like a dream for me.

Before meeting you on 11th March, I had everything in my life except LOVE and PASSION.

When we started chatting, I was looking for a lady who could support me in all aspects.

And when I met you on 8th April, it was like a dream come true.

I never get such warmth, emotional touch, and passionate LOVE.

You are such a sweet darling with whom I would like to be with, all my days and all my nights. I have read that our earth has 'force of gravity' which forces all things to fall, but you have more 'force of gravity' than earth which is forcing me to fall for you and that also forever. You're the best thing that ever happened to me. That's why I love you so much.

I remember the first time I saw you at the airport, and I couldn't believe just how beautiful you were, and still are. By this, I mean your personality - your sense of humour, your intelligence and how easily you can express yourself. I have always found it particularly difficult, but you made me feel comfortable, safe, and happy.

You are not only my girlfriend; you are my best friend; my soul mate. You're the first person I want to tell my news to - good or bad. You're the first person I go to when I need comfort, a cuddle, and a kiss. You make me smile, and I hope I make you feel the same way too because you deserve it, and so much more.

Today when you told me about your dream of honeymoon, I was so happy and excited that I didn't even think that it would hurt you. I told you that we are running too fast. I know you got hurt. I felt your sadness; maybe your eyes were wet. On that moment, I wish I could hold you until the tears stop filling up your eyes. I wish I could just wrap my arms around you and tell you that we will go for our honeymoon, and everything will be okay in the end. I wish you could just believe me when I tell you how much I care for you and that I'm not going to run away, because I love you.

When we go for our honeymoon, I want the weather to be freezing temperatures, so that it gives me every excuse to hold you in my arms, to keep you warm. I have cold hands, so maybe you could hold them close to your heart to heat them because I've never met someone so warm-hearted and as kind as you. I'm so lucky to have you in my life. Thanks for everything you have given me till now.

'Teri Meri Prem Kahani do Lafzon main Bayan na ho paye'

With lots of love and kisses.

Yours'

Raj

The second letter from Raj.

Good morning, my love...

I know that there is nothing better than waking up with you in mind, even after having spent the night thinking about you. I'm much happier since the day I met you. Our first glance, our first hug, our first kiss made the miracle of our love to be born on that special date (8th) when we celebrate our first day together.

This feeling of always wanting to stay connected with you day and night, through some excuse, whether it's a phone call or a chat—I've never felt this way before, and I won't be able to feel this for anyone else in the future. It's only you, only you, for whom I wait while awake, and for whom I wait even in my sleep. And this didn't just happen—it's something I've waited many years for, and finally, YOU have come into my life, and I have found your love, and I am really thankful to GOD for that.

You know, after meeting you, I've realised what LOVE truly is. Every moment, your love-filled eyes keep watching me... every moment, the scent of your body lingers around me, and I can feel it nearby... it feels like you're right here, close to me. For me, no one can ever be more beautiful or more loving than you, and that's why I will only wish from GOD that you always stay with me, very close to me, in my arms, with the truth that our love for each other will never fade.

I love you and always will. I feel like this love will last even when maturity comes, forever and ever. I'm sure someone up there is watching (and enjoying;)) for this beautiful relation we have. Since we met, I feel much more sentimental. In my mind, there are only images of my beautiful Meghna. When I recall that first kiss, I know that was the great and definite moment, the kiss of my loved one... that perfect moment is being remembered today, and I can only feel love and happiness in my heart because of it. When we first kissed, that was by far the most intense minutes of our romance, undoubtedly the happiest day of my life... Truly unforgettable indeed.

I would like to live that moment again and again and again...

Your's

Raj

The third letter from Raj.

I believe that we are made for each other. God bless both of us.

With the world's precious and eternal feeling, that is Love...

Nobody understands that there are so many things we cannot see or hear,

Measure or count, which affects our lives very much, cannot be described.

For example, we breathe in oxygen, and it's very important for us too, but we can't see it.

In a same way we cannot see, hear or measure the feelings of love, but it's there in our heart.

Same way in our relationship, this love is also spread like oxygen in the air... so I love you and need you same as I need oxygen to live... Muuuaaaahh.

Yours

Raj

The fourth letter from Raj

Dear *Biwi ji*, (My dear Wife),

This morning, after talking to you, I got onto the boat... carrying your memories with me. This time, every moment we spent together, I kept the memory of those moments in my heart. When I sat in the boat, it felt like my boat wasn't sailing on the waves of the sea, but rather floating on the blue sky's blanket. And in that boat, it didn't feel like anyone else was there; it just felt like it was only YOU and ME....

The feeling of love that you've made me experience was once a dream for me... I used to wonder, the kind of love I read about in books or see in films, if that kind of love is real, I didn't know when I'd ever find it... Then we met... we met many times... but perhaps due to a lack of time, we couldn't spend much time together. But this time, after meeting you and spending some time with you, that dream of mine came true... In fact, you could say I received even more than a dream. And for that, I won't thank you, but I will definitely thank God... who brought us together and set this time for us to spend together. I LOVE YOU VERY MUCH... muuuuahhhhhh!!!

"As you say, 'Who knows what tomorrow holds'... I also believe that no one knows about tomorrow, but after meeting you, my faith in God has only strengthened. I know that whatever He does, it will be for the best. It is by His blessing that we met, and He will protect our relationship. No one will be able to come between us, even if they try. For me, the word 'LOVE' begins and ends with you. That's why the last 6 days have been the most beautiful days of my life, and I will always cherish these moments with me until my last breath" Love you so much...

Your's

Raj

Chapter XII

When love remains even after a relationship ends, it speaks to the depth and purity of that emotion. Such love is not dependent on physical presence or the continuation of the relationship but is rooted in the connection shared and the growth experienced together. Here's a breakdown of the emotions involved when love endures beyond the end of a relationship:

1. Unconditional Affection

    - The love that lingers after a relationship has ended often becomes unconditional. It transcends expectations or desires for reciprocity, existing simply because it was a genuine and heartfelt emotion. You care for the person, wish them well, and hope they find happiness, even if it's no longer with you.

2. Gratitude and Memories

    - The emotional bond remains through the memories shared. Even though the relationship may be over, the experiences, moments of joy, and growth remain imprinted in your heart. You feel grateful for the love you once had, recognising the value it brought to your life, even if the circumstances or timing didn't allow it to last.

3. Emotional Maturity

    • Love that persists after a breakup often reflects emotional maturity. It's the realisation that sometimes relationships end not because of a lack of love, but because of other factors— timing, personal growth, life circumstances. Accepting this truth allows the love to evolve into something less possessive, where you hold on to the emotion without clinging to the person.

4. Selflessness

    • When love remains despite the end of a relationship, there's a selflessness in it. You may no longer be involved in the other person's life, but you still want the best for them. It's about accepting that love doesn't have to equate to being together. True love means letting go, when necessary, even while keeping the feeling in your heart.

5. Personal Growth

    • Often, the love that stays with you is a testament to the impact the relationship had on your personal growth. Whether the relationship was fulfilling, challenging, or both, it shaped you in significant ways. This lasting love is an acknowledgement of how the connection helped you grow, learn about yourself, and evolve emotionally.

6. Forgiveness and Peace

    • After the end of a relationship, if love remains, it often comes with a sense of forgiveness and peace. There's an understanding that both people did their best with what they knew at the time. Instead of harbouring resentment or bitterness, this lingering love brings a calm acceptance of the past.

7. Enduring Connection

- Sometimes, love that remains is tied to the unique connection you shared. Even if circumstances change, the bond feels timeless. It's not about wanting the relationship back, but more about acknowledging that a part of you will always hold space for that person because of what they meant to you.

8. Freedom from Attachment

- When love endures after a relationship has ended, it becomes free from attachment. You no longer need the person to be physically present or involved in your life for the love to exist. It's no longer bound by expectations or the relationship's formalities. Instead, it becomes a pure emotion that stays with you without causing pain or longing.

In essence, when love remains after the relationship is over, it reflects a deep emotional connection that wasn't dependent on external conditions. It's love in its truest form—one that transcends the boundaries of time, circumstances, and physical presence, allowing both people to move forward while holding onto the beauty of what once was.

The butterflies may not fly anymore, but the sensation never died.

The End

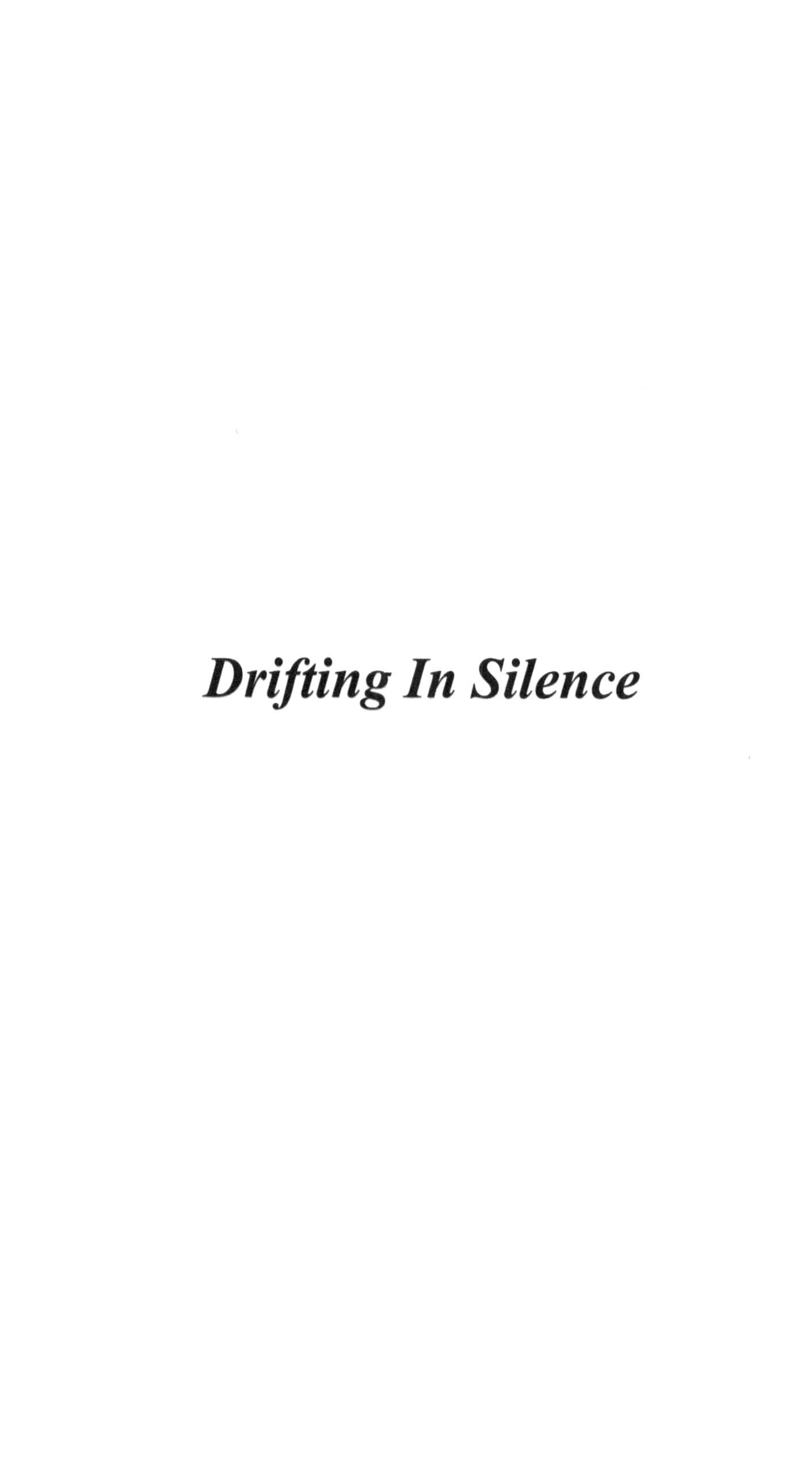

Drifting In Silence

Chapter I

The mobile phone is showing the time; it's 12:02 am, midnight.

Massages received...

You got married, right?

On 23rd June?

Tell me?

What?

The mobile phone is showing the time as 01:07 AM, midnight

Now you are married, aren't you?

Call me

I am awake

What's that, why is my cell phone sending so many notifications in the middle of the night? Okay, these are WhatsApp messages, who is sending all these now?

Nandini was in a deep sleep when she was woken by the constant buzzing of message notifications on her phone. Still half-asleep, she reached for her phone to check if there was anything urgent from her daughter or husband, as both were in different cities. In fact, all three of them were currently in three different cities.

Oh! It's Aakash! Is he crazy? Why is he sending messages in the middle of the night? Forget it; I need to get some sleep. I'm not replying to this nonsense at this hour, Nandini thinks.

The cell phone started beeping again.

I want to talk to you.

Call me

Hello

What happened

Call

Are you with someone?

Okay

Hello

Call me

Nandini found it impossible to sleep now. What does he want? Who tries to talk to someone in the middle of the night? Frustrated, she switched on the bedside lamp and reached for her glasses—her eyesight wasn't as sharp as it used to be. Age was catching up.

She began typing a reply: *'What is this, Aakash? Who messages at midnight? If you want to talk, come see me tomorrow after work, as I'll be leaving the day after tomorrow. Now, please let me sleep. I've taken sleeping pills, and it's hard for me to talk or text right now.'*

No

Wait

You have to talk to me.

Now

You are now married, right?

Bipasha showed me your picture that you got married. Is it true?

Why are you hiding

Listen

I am drunk

I can't text properly.

Nandini glanced at the clock again—it was 1:35 a.m. *My goodness,* she thought *this man is out of his mind. He doesn't sleep, and he won't let me sleep either.*

Frustrated, she decided to reply one last time: 'I have never hidden anything from anyone, why should I? Good night', she wrote and hit send.

Okay

I drank a full bottle

If you allow me to meet with Bipasha, then let me know.

Otherwise, I can't meet you alone.

Bye bye

Be happy

Nandini just lost her patience now. She texts Aakash again

"Are you going mad? If you can't meet me alone, then forget it. Honestly, you don't even have the courage to face me by yourself after the mess you created. If you ever find the bravery, even if it takes you 5-10 years, then come and meet me—but only alone."

Aakash again started texting

Why don't you meet Bipasha?

She is your friend now, right?

You guys share everything with each other.

Then, why don't you allow me to meet you with her.

Hello

Talk to me

Call me

I can't text

I can't see anything now

I am feeling drowsy.

"I have told you, I have made my last call with you already. It's 2:00 am now. Please let me sleep for a few hours. I have to go to the office in the morning," Nandini replied.

Okay

Go to sleep

Don't bother about me.

I don't need anyone.

Good night

Bye bye.

Nandini tries to sleep again, but her mind is racing with too many thoughts. She's battling to fall asleep but just can't.

Another reason for this visit was to meet Aakash one last time. Everything that happened between them had only been through phone calls and text messages. It was Bipasha who made all the calls and initiated contact, even arranging a meeting when Nandini realised the depth of the damage Bipasha had caused, not Aakash. Bipasha did everything in her power to ensure that Nandini would never return to Aakash's life. What a tragedy!

The purpose of the meeting was to give the best possible closure to a 15-year-long relationship, but that wasn't achieved. Fifteen long years is almost a decade. Nandini knows this unresolved ending will haunt them for the rest of their lives. Closure is essential for moving forward on their separate paths.

Nandini didn't want to dwell on it any longer. If Adarsh (her husband) found out that she called her ex-boyfriend at 2 a.m., he would surely be upset. They had only been married for two months, and this was both of their second marriages. Nandini had been open about her past and her relationship with Aakash. Adarsh was a gentle, caring, mature, and humble person who valued Nandini's emotions and thoughts. As she contemplated their future together, she realised the importance of maintaining transparency in their relationship; she didn't want any further complications in her life.

Anyway, Nandini muted her phone and tried to sleep, as it was now 2:30 a.m. In the morning, she had to rush to the office by 10 a.m. since tomorrow was her last day. She had a lot of things to wrap up.

Chapter II

Nandini Chatterjee is a dignified 45-year-old professional, working as a project manager for a multinational corporation. Her job requires her to travel frequently within the country. She remarried just two months ago and has a daughter from her previous marriage. Her first husband passed away when their daughter was only two years old. Since then, Nandini has taken on all the financial responsibilities to ensure her daughter's upbringing.

Her head office was in Delhi at that time, but due to her frequent travel, she couldn't take full responsibility for her child. As a result, her daughter mostly stays with her grandparents—Nandini's parents. After her husband's death, Nandini returned from her in-laws' house, as they had always blamed her for his passing. She has not kept in touch with them since.

Nandini left her hometown when she was just 28 years old and struggled a lot over the years. During one of her business trips, she met Aakash in a casual encounter while travelling. She discovered that he also lived in the same city, was unmarried, and was staying in a boys' hostel since he had moved to Delhi for work at a news channel.

Nandini didn't find anything particularly interesting in Aakash; he was an average-looking, quiet guy. They exchanged a few formal conversations while sitting together and decided to exchange phone numbers in case there were any future updates, since they lived in the same city.

Time passed as it always does, and Nandini never even attempted to contact Aakash; in fact, she almost forgot about him. There were so many people we meet along our journey, and it's just a coincidence how few of them we truly remember. Nandini had no intention of making friends or pursuing any relationships. She was always occupied with her work, striving for the best possible results. Her sole focus was on building a successful career to provide all the facilities for her daughter, ensuring she would never feel deprived as a child of a single parent. She didn't even think for a second about marriage.

One day, after six long months, as she was preparing to head out for a meeting in the city around 4 o'clock, her phone buzzed with a text message. Knowing she had a long journey ahead, she took out her mobile and checked the notification. To her surprise, it was a message from Mr. Aakash Yadav. She paused, trying to recall who he was, when suddenly a vivid image of his face flashed before her eyes. "Ah, I remember now," she thought, a smile spreading across her face. As she read the message, laughter bubbled up within her.

The message read, "Today is my birthday, and no one has wished me yet."

She knew instantly that it was a flirty message, even though he had never mentioned his birthday before. Smiling to herself, she decided to play along. She replied, "Oh, it's good to know today is your birthday! Many happy returns of the day. We'll catch up soon, and I'll make sure to get that party from you too. Take care!"

This was the first message that originated from Aakash and after that, almost every day, they kept messaging each other. Another month went this way. One sudden Sunday, Aakash asked Nandi to meet somewhere in the evening for tea/coffee.

Nandini had formed the impression from their chat messages that he was a decent guy, and she saw no harm in meeting him for a coffee. After all, she often felt lonely after work, and the idea of some casual company seemed appealing. There were days when the weight of her solitude became heavier, especially when she thought about her daughter, whom she couldn't keep with her. That lingering guilt and sadness made the prospect of a brief distraction, like a coffee meeting, seem harmless and even comforting.

They arranged to meet at 7 p.m. at Malviya Nagar, South Delhi. It was convenient for both—Nandini lived in the area, while Aakash stayed in a boys' hostel nearby in South Extension. Nandini arrived on time, waiting in front of a well-known sweets shop, and Aakash showed up about ten minutes later. As he approached, she noticed he was riding a striking yellow motorcycle, sleek and stylish, clearly the kind that turns heads. It was very much in fashion. Aakash himself matched the impression—tall, handsome, and undeniably attractive.

Nandini couldn't help but think, *Wah! Not bad,* as she admired Aakash and his motorcycle. However, a wave of hesitation washed over her. She had never ridden on a motorcycle with someone she didn't know well, and the idea made her a little uneasy. Sensing her discomfort, Aakash quickly understood her reluctance. But with no other way to get to their destination, she decided to give it a try.

Carefully, she mounted the bike, making sure to maintain as little contact with Aakash as possible, her hesitation lingering in every movement.

Nandini had no clue that Aakash saw their meeting as their first date. For her, it was just a casual coffee outing with an acquaintance, nothing more. She viewed it as a simple way to pass the time, a friendly chat over coffee, while Aakash had something entirely different in mind. Unbeknownst to her, he had already started to see this as the beginning of something more meaningful.

Nandini saw Aakash as nothing more than a good friend—someone who spoke very little but came across as mature and responsible. During their conversation, Aakash casually asked if she had visited many of the local spots in Delhi. Nandini admitted that she hadn't had the time, and besides, she didn't really have a friend to explore the city with. The thought of discovering Delhi with someone else had never crossed her mind, as her days were often consumed with work and personal responsibilities.

Aakash suggested they explore the city together, thinking it could be a great way to help her feel more comfortable in an unfamiliar place with someone new. What had started as a simple coffee date in Nandini's mind slowly shifted into something more. Instead of just coffee, they ended up having dinner at the well-known spot, Delhi Hut, in South Delhi. The evening unfolded naturally, with good conversation and a relaxed atmosphere. After dinner, Aakash politely dropped her off at her place and headed back, leaving Nandini to reflect on how the evening had turned out differently than she had imagined.

Nandini found Aakash to be well-mannered, with a good sense of gesture. He may not have been particularly attractive to her, but he seemed decent enough. However, as the evening progressed, she realised that her feelings toward him wouldn't go beyond casual friendship. Aakash, though kind, wasn't like her. Nandini saw herself as a flowing river—dynamic, free-spirited, and always moving. Aakash, on the other hand, felt more like water in a reserved tank—steady, contained, and lacking the same sense of spontaneity. It became clear to her that while they could be friends, they were fundamentally different at their core.

But who are we to decide our fate? Everything is already destined. Nandini couldn't help but reflect on this thought. Despite her realisations about their differences, she understood that life often has its own way of unfolding, beyond what we plan or expect. Perhaps there was a reason for Aakash's presence in her life, even if it wasn't clear at the moment. Fate, after all, works in mysterious ways, often leading us down paths we never anticipated.

Chapter III

After dropping Nandini at her place, Aakash returned to his boys' hostel and began texting her. Their conversation continued for another two hours. As they messaged back and forth, they began to share more personal details, slowly building a bridge between them. Both were lonely in the city, far from their families, and this connection seemed to ease that sense of isolation. Nandini soon realised that Aakash felt more comfortable communicating through texts than face-to-face conversations.

Before long, they developed a habit of chatting every day after work, often for hours. Their growing bond also led to regular weekend meetups, and whenever they had time after work, they would find moments to see each other in person. What began as casual interactions had evolved into a shared routine, filling the gaps of loneliness for both of them.

Aakash began to take Nandini to different places around the city, and with each outing, she found herself enjoying his company more and more. They explored new cafés, parks, and local attractions, sharing laughter and stories along the way. Despite the growing camaraderie, Nandini never allowed herself to entertain any deeper feelings for Aakash. She viewed their relationship as a friendship, appreciating the companionship without the complications of romance. Each day brought them closer, but in her heart, she remained grounded in her perception of him as just a good friend.

Time moved at its own pace, and gradually, a warm bond formed between Aakash and Nandini. One day, after two months had passed, Nandini felt she could trust Aakash because of his kind and reliable nature. As a thoughtful gesture, she decided to invite him to her rented home for lunch or dinner, whichever suited him best. Aakash happily accepted her invitation, and they planned to meet for lunch on a Sunday.

Nandini prepared Aakash's favourite dish—egg curry with rice. Since Aakash had been staying in a boys' hostel and mostly ate fast food or meals from outside, he really appreciated the home-cooked meal, saying it had been a long time since he had such comforting food. Nandini felt happy knowing she could do something meaningful to show her appreciation.

Aakash arrived a bit late, so they ended up finishing lunch around 3:30 PM. Afterward, Nandini suggested he take some rest, and they both sat together, listening to music in a relaxed mood. Time seemed to slip away, and before Nandini realised it, the room had grown dark along with the outside. As she got up to turn on the light, Aakash gently pulled her back onto the sofa and, without warning, began kissing her.

Nandini, 28 years old, had been emotionally starved for the last two years after her husband's death. She was caught off guard by Aakash's sudden move, but since she had also developed feelings for him, she didn't feel the need to stop him. Instead, she found herself enjoying his cuddling, hugging, and kissing, giving in to the moment.

From that evening, Nandini and Aakash began a new journey together. However, neither of them ever spoke openly about falling in love, either before or after that moment. They didn't make any official declaration or announcement that they were in love; it was simply understood between them, unspoken but felt deeply.

Aakash left after an hour, but Nandini was left in confusion, unsure of what had really happened between them. She couldn't figure out where their relationship was headed. Was it an expression of love, or simply a moment of physical intimacy between two mature people caught up in the heat of the moment? The uncertainty lingered, leaving her with more questions than answers.

A few days passed, and surprisingly, Aakash neither called nor messaged Nandini. She rarely called or messaged him, only when there was an emergency. But this time, she couldn't help but wonder if he was avoiding her because of what happened the last time they met. Maybe he felt awkward or something else was bothering him. Knowing Aakash lived alone in a boys' hostel, she also started worrying if he was alright. Deciding not to overthink, she made up her mind to call him after work.

In the evening, after returning home from work, Nandini called Aakash. It was around 8 p.m. She tried twice, but he didn't answer. Her worry deepened—was he okay? There was no other way for her to find out any news about him.

Chapter IV

After a week, Nandini suddenly got a call from Aakash in the evening. She was surprised and worried, asking if he was okay or if something had happened because he hadn't called to let her know. Aakash apologised for not contacting her. He explained that he had to go on an unexpected outdoor shoot, and because of poor network and being surrounded by people, he couldn't call her.

Nandini was a bit surprised and thought Aakash was trying to distance himself from her out of guilt. She asked if he was still out of town or if he had returned and if he wanted to meet. Aakash said he came back the night before but might not be able to meet because of work. Nandini realised Aakash was trying to avoid her.

After a few days, Nandini and Aakash started getting back to normal. They began chatting over the phone again at night. Nandini felt the need to talk about their relationship, so she asked him to meet her, this time outside, like they used to in the past.

Aakash picked Nandini up from her office, and they went out for dinner.

"Is there anything you want to tell me?" Nandini asked Aakash directly.

Aakash was busy setting the table instead of answering her, avoiding eye contact. Nandini found it a little amusing. She knew Aakash couldn't easily express himself; it wasn't in his nature.

As usual, Aakash avoided the conversation. They finished their meal, and Aakash dropped Nandini home. She invited him upstairs for coffee, but Aakash politely refused and left.

After Aakash reached home, he called Nandini.

"I'm sorry for how I acted that evening," he said softly.

Nandini smiled gently and replied, "Why are you apologising? We're both mature, and what happened that day was mutual. You don't need to feel guilty." Her calm voice tried to ease his discomfort.

Aakash sighed and continued, "Nandini, I like you, but my family, especially my mother, won't accept us. She's old-fashioned. Even though she's a widow herself, she can't imagine her son marrying a widow—especially one with a child. I feel guilty because I know this is the real reason we can't continue this relationship."

Nandini smiled quietly. So that was the source of his guilt. "Aakash, you don't need to apologise for that. What happened between us was mutual, and it was nice. I never expected anything in return. And if you're asking me about marriage, I can't offer that. I've been married once, and I have a child now. My focus is on my career. So please, don't worry about me."

Aakash seemed relieved but still hesitant. "Are you sure, Nandini? I don't want you to feel hurt later because I can't make any commitments."

"Yes, Aakash, I'm sure. Please don't worry about me. It's better you find someone who matches your family's expectations and settle down."

"I don't want to marry," Aakash blurted out suddenly.

Nandini was surprised. "Why not, Aakash? Can you tell me?"

He took a deep breath. "I had a girlfriend back in college. I couldn't commit to her then because I didn't have a job, and life was so uncertain. But I loved her, though I didn't realise it until after we separated. Six months after we broke up, I started feeling a deep connection, hoping she'd reach out. But she never did. Last month, just after meeting you, I received her wedding invitation. That's when I knew—I'll never get married. She should know she's the reason for that."

Aakash spoke quickly, as if releasing a weight he had been carrying for too long.

Nandini listened carefully, surprised by his story. "First love is always hard to forget," she said softly. "It sounds like you still have feelings for her."

"I'm sorry to say this, Nandini, but I believe one only truly falls in love once in life. Everything else is just a compromise," Aakash replied, his voice innocent but firm.

Nandini couldn't agree. "Do you really think a person can only love once in their whole life?" she asked gently, her heart not ready to accept his view.

Aakash simply nodded, "Yes, I think so."

Nandini decided not to argue. She realised that while they might share a special bond, perhaps as close friends or well-wishers, Aakash didn't seem interested in taking their relationship seriously.

After the serious discussion, Nandini also felt that she shouldn't expect this relationship to become something deeper. Wanting to lighten the mood, she asked Aakash to play some of their favourite old songs, just like they used to.

Aakash started his record player. Nandini listened over the phone, and as the music played, the melody slowly softened the tension in the room.

Half an hour later, around midnight, Nandini drifted off to sleep, feeling more at peace.

Chapter V

Nandini had been on a work trip for the past few days when Aakash called her during office hours to help her with some details about her upcoming move to a new apartment. Aakash had taken on nearly every responsibility for Nandini now. Though they hadn't formally married, they were connected at a deeper, soulful level. Aakash handled everything for her, and when she introduced him as her husband for the new accommodation, it felt natural. He no longer hesitated.

Even though they didn't live together, Aakash would visit Nandini's place regularly, and they spent weekends together. Nandini felt assured that, despite the absence of any formal or verbal commitment, Aakash wasn't going to leave her. Some things don't need to be written or spoken—they just exist through understanding.

One day, Aakash called and said, "Hi Nandini, how are you? Should we plan a short 3-4 day trip near Delhi once you're back?"

They had been dating for nine months, and during that time, Nandini had come to see Aakash as caring, protective, and sweet, though he didn't talk much. "Yes, why not? That sounds like a great idea," Nandini replied.

A few days after returning to Delhi, they both went to Shimla in January. Shimla, with its snowy mountains and chilled climate, was a perfect escape. It was their first trip together as a couple, and they enjoyed every moment—candlelight, wine, the beauty of the hills—it was all magical. After four days, they returned to their everyday lives, but something had shifted in their relationship.

Aakash became even more caring and thoughtful towards Nandini. Although they didn't meet every day, they spent hours talking on the phone after work—sometimes for 2-3 hours. Aakash started opening up, sharing his family history, struggles, and personal matters. Nandini realised that beneath his quiet exterior, Aakash was a lonely soul, an introvert who only shared his feelings once he found his comfort zone.

Things were going smoothly for Nandini. She had recently changed jobs, securing a pay raise, which was crucial for her as a single mother. One evening, Aakash invited her for a dinner date. Nandini was excited and came home from work a little early, dressing up in a beautiful saree with matching accessories. It was February, during the coldest part of the year in Delhi, when the city is often blanketed in fog, making it hard to tell day from night.

Aakash arrived on time, riding his sleek yellow motorcycle. He handed her a bouquet of flowers, a box of chocolates, and a greeting card. Nandini was taken by surprise and didn't know what to make of it. Aakash stepped closer, leaned in, and whispered in her ear, "Happy Valentine's Day, Nandini." He then kissed her forehead, followed by a soft kiss on her lips.

Nandini was stunned. She had never seen this side of Aakash before and never expected him to express his feelings like that. It was the first time in her life that someone had given her red roses on

Valentine's Day. Speechless, she wondered to herself, is this what love feels like? Has Aakash finally fallen in love with her?

Aakash surprised Nandini with a romantic candlelight dinner. Though she had been out for dinner many times before, this evening felt different, exceeding her every expectation. After their meal, they returned home together, where Aakash gave her the gift of a truly enchanting night. Nandini felt as if she were living in a fairy tale, cherished as the princess of her prince. When Aakash whispered those long-awaited words, "I love you," Nandini was overwhelmed with emotion, her tears flowing freely. She had yearned to hear them for years. Although they had shared moments of physical love before, this time was different—infused with the tenderness of emotional connection, it transcended into something divine. Her eyes filled with tears as she gazed at Aakash, melting into his arms, ready to stay there forever.

Aakash came to see Nandini again after seven days. During that time, they had spoken often over the phone – they laughed, they cried, and they healed together. As soon as she saw him, Nandini smiled, hugged him, and asked, "Love can happen later too, right?"

Aakash felt a bit uneasy, remembering why she asked that. Nine months ago, he had told her that true love only happens once in a lifetime.

"Yes, Nandini, you were right. Love can happen later too. And it's not a compromise," he replied softly.

Nandini felt fortunate to have found love again. Being in love is one of the most beautiful experiences in life. The only challenge was that Aakash spoke very little and rarely expressed his feelings. He was never demanding; he just acted on what he felt in the moment. Nandini had come to accept that Aakash wasn't the romantic type

– he didn't often share his emotions with words, but his actions always spoke louder.

People may drift apart over time, but some memories stay with us forever—especially those sweet moments that make the past unforgettable.

Nandini's new apartment was a cosy little space, with just one bedroom, a combined living and dining area, a kitchen, an attached bathroom, and a small balcony. The bedroom had a full glass wall, and since the apartment was on the top floor, it offered a breathtaking view of the night sky. From her bed, Nandini could gaze out at the vast expanse above—sometimes illuminated by a glowing full moon, other times dotted with a blanket of stars. It felt as if she were peering into the galaxy through a glass panel. On sleepless nights, when she was alone, she would spend hours simply watching the stars, lost in the beauty of the Milky Way.

But beneath the calm of those starry nights, Nandini often felt a deep ache in her heart. She missed her daughter, only four years old, whom she had to leave in the care of her parents. As a mother, the helplessness she felt was overwhelming. She yearned for the joy of witnessing her child grow up before her eyes, but that experience had been taken from her. Nandini's tears soaked her pillow as she grieved for the moments she had missed—the tender, irreplaceable feelings of motherhood she longed to embrace.

Sometimes, Aakash could sense Nandini's hidden pain. Whenever they were together, he would try to lift her mood. One night, after they had shared an intimate moment, they lay in bed, gazing at the sky through the glass wall. It was a full moon night, but Nandini seemed lost in her own thoughts, distant. Aakash understood her silence. Gently, he began humming the tune, "तेरे बिना ज़िन्दगी में कोई शिकवा तो नहीं... शिकवा नहीं..."

Nandini knew the song wasn't just for her; Aakash was singing for his first love, someone he still missed from time to time. Some nights hold an undeniable weight, a heaviness we all feel at times.

Suddenly, Aakash stopped singing. He looked at Nandini's face, then back at the full moon, and then at her again.

Curious, Nandini asked, "What's going on? What are you staring at?"

Aakash smiled and replied, "Tonight, you look incredibly beautiful. I'm just trying to decide which is more beautiful—the moon or you. Because honestly, you've never looked this stunning before."

Nandini burst into laughter, her heart lighter, the moment filled with joy. Some memories are never forgotten.

Chapter VI

It's been three years now. Many changes happened in between. Aakash got a good opportunity and now he holds a senior position in his office. Nandini also got promotions. Both of them are financially a little uplifted. The most important thing is Aakash moved on from his boys' hostel. His mother shifted to Noida as she got retainment after a long struggle for bringing up her 3 kids. Now Aakash stayed with his family. They took a rented house. Aakash, his younger brother, his younger sister and his mother. His sister prepared herself for cracking IS exam. Aakash couldn't stay with Nandini for the whole weekend as he felt obligation from his family.

Now, Aakash would often come to Nandini's place for the day and stay the night very often. Nandini had also moved to a slightly bigger apartment. Her parents would visit once a year, bringing her daughter with them, and they would stay for 15 days. Nandini would also travel to her hometown once a year to see her daughter and parents. So, she was able to spend about 15-20 days with her daughter twice a year. Over time, her parents became aware of Aakash's presence in her life. After meeting him, they felt a bit relieved, knowing there was someone looking after Nandini.

Nandini's father even suggested sending a marriage proposal to Aakash's family on her behalf, but she refused. There were many reasons for this decision. At one point, Nandini visited Aakash's family out of courtesy and realised that Aakash had no desire to get married. She knew that if they tried to marry, they wouldn't be truly happy. Over the years, Nandini had come to understand that Aakash was different from others—he had his own world and fiercely guarded his privacy. He could be a great friend, a well-wisher, but he was not meant to be a life partner. If Nandini tried to force the relationship into marriage, the beautiful bond they shared could be destroyed.

Moreover, in India, marriage isn't just between two individuals; it involves the entire family of the groom. With that came a lot of responsibilities, and Nandini knew that if she married Aakash, her career could suffer. She wasn't willing to compromise on that. She had struggled for herself and for her daughter's future and couldn't afford to be selfish.

One of the hardest truths in life is that a child rarely receives the same care and affection from a step-parent as they would from their biological parent. Nandini understood this well.

This time Nandini planned for going out for 2-3 days from Delhi. Due to their hectic schedule, Nandini and Aakash couldn't make time for themselves. So Nandini thought that spending quality time would be a nice idea to uplift their relationship. Nandini planned to go to Rishikesh and Mussoorie.

Aakash agreed and they went to Rishikesh first. Aakash said one of his friends recommended the hotel as it was situated on the bank of the river Ganga. The place was very beautiful, with a river view from their room. But suddenly, Nandini smelled something unusual. She felt afraid, started checking all over, and then she went outside their room. On the bank of the river, they burned the dead bodies openly. Nandini was shocked as she hadn't had this experience before. Also, the burning smell of the human body was so intolerable that she asked Aakash to change the hotel as soon as possible. But Aakash didn't agree to that. Nandini was very upset with the choice and was trying to adjust to that uncomfortable situation.

Nandini had no idea that it was a sign from the universe—sometimes smoke is just a warning of the fire that is yet to come in life.

This time, Nandini noticed a clear change in Aakash's behaviour. He seemed distant, avoiding physical contact and remained silent most of the time, only texting someone on his phone. Nandini felt as though she had come on this trip alone. Although Aakash was physically present, his mind and attention were elsewhere. Being a keen observer, Nandini began to notice more changes in him. Aakash was staying up all night, even after Nandini had gone to bed, and slept through most of the day, which was unusual and uncomfortable for her to accept.

One day, while Aakash was asleep during the day, Nandini took the chance to check his phone. To her shock, she discovered that all of Aakash's texts were to a woman named Namrita. Although the messages weren't particularly emotional, they detailed his activities—like visiting places alone and giving a vivid description of what he did. Nandini read through the messages quietly, not saying anything, and decided to wait for the right moment to confront him.

She pushed through the rest of the three-day trip, regretting her decision to come with Aakash. She felt completely lost, as if someone had thrown her into an abyss. Nandini stopped speaking to Aakash, and it didn't take long for him to realise something was wrong.

On their way back to Delhi, Aakash insisted she tell him what was bothering her. They were travelling by train during the day, surrounded by people. Suddenly, Nandini broke down in tears, feeling utterly betrayed by Aakash. He was unprepared for her emotional outburst and desperately tried to cover his tracks, making up fake stories to calm her down, aware that they were in a public place. But the more he tried to explain, the worse the situation became.

Eventually, Aakash gave up and confessed the truth – he had a new "girlfriend" he had been talking to over the phone. He swore he would never contact her again and even took an oath, promising that he would never repeat the mistake.

Chapter VII

Nandini returned to Delhi, but life as she knew it had changed forever. Her trust in Aakash had been shattered. To her, once someone lies, it's hard to see them the same way again. Even though she decided to continue her relationship with Aakash, it was different now—distant and guarded. The complication was that she had introduced Aakash as her husband, though they had never lived together. She had done this because of her social security issues, and in times of emergency, he was still the only person she could count on. They had invested so many years in their relationship, and that history held them together.

Aakash understood the gravity of his mistake and how deeply it hurt Nandini. He tried hard to make things right, apologising over and over again. Nandini, conflicted, decided to give him a second chance. But things weren't the same. Aakash became overly cautious—never leaving his phone unattended, even taking it with him to the bathroom. This secretive behaviour unsettled Nandini, and suspicion grew in her heart. Yet, feeling helpless, she chose to ignore it, hoping that things would eventually fall back into place. But deep down, she knew the trust had faded.

Time passed, but the emotional distance between them lingered. Another two years slipped by. Aakash still visited Nandini every weekend, but the connection between them felt like it had disappeared. Their relationship had become a routine, one Nandini followed without confrontation or argument. She knew in her heart that there was nothing left between them but habits.

Aakash, on the other hand, threw himself into a new business venture, alongside his job, nurturing his love for plants. He dragged Nandini along to plant group meetings and flower shows, as if trying to fill the gap in their relationship. They both had only one day off a week, but after a while, Nandini grew tired of these outings and began to decline his invitations. As Aakash's business prospered, he bought himself a new car, but the old yellow motorbike in the garage still stood—a silent witness to the past, its once-vivid memories now fading into the background.

As the saying goes, the universe doesn't allow emptiness for long. Nandini became almost certain that Aakash had other women in his life. She began doing things on her own—shopping, watching movies, dining out—all without Aakash. His absence was now glaringly obvious.

As the years passed, Nandini found herself more settled in her career. She felt stronger, learning that life teaches everything if you're willing to listen. She no longer sought emotional support from anyone. She realised that healing in peace was far more important than relying on others. She made new friends, and her colleagues became a source of comfort and affection. But Aakash still visited her every weekend, and they continued their hollow routine—spending time together, having sex without the warmth of affection. He would call her every night on his way home, just like before.

Then, one day, while sitting in her office, Nandini had a moment of clarity. Why did she need a man in her life when she was fully capable of handling everything on her own? She was financially stable, her daughter was thriving, studying for her bachelor's degree in a prestigious college, and Nandini felt secure in her independence.

With a calm heart, she typed a message to Aakash: "Dear Aakash, I feel grateful for everything you've done for me. We've shared many beautiful moments together. But I want to stop now. There's nothing left between us. I hope you understand my decision and accept it with maturity. Thank you."

Aakash didn't call her during office hours, but he did call her right after receiving the message. He was shocked, of course. It's not every day that someone ends things so definitively. But Nandini had made up her mind.

This was her time—to break free, to live life on her own terms, and to finally let go of what no longer served her.

Chapter VIII

Six months passed by. At first, Aakash tried calling Nandini a few times, but he never visited her place again after receiving her message. Nandini had expected he might come by—it had been over ten years of him visiting her every week. Despite everything, Aakash had never married, but he never showed up again. Sometimes, Nandini quietly smiled to herself, feeling reassured that she had made the right decision. She only wished she had made it sooner.

Yet, there were moments when Nandini missed Aakash deeply. Over the years, she had grown used to his presence in her life. The truth is, when you spend a long time with someone, even if it's not perfect, you become attached—just like with a pet. It's human nature to get used to companionship, no matter what.

Then, in March 2020, the pandemic hit India. Life came to a sudden halt. Everything stopped for months, and people were forced to stay inside their homes. This unexpected shift threw everyone into a different reality, full of fear and uncertainty. Panic spread, and the fear of death loomed large. No one knew how to battle this invisible virus, COVID-19. Every industry shut down, except for healthcare and the media.

It was a tough time for everyone. Nandini lived alone in her apartment, and the isolation weighed on her. One day, overwhelmed by the circumstances, she picked up the phone and called Aakash. Her landlords lived in the same building and were very caring, but they were also frightened by the pandemic. They knew Nandini was married, or so they believed, and assumed her husband was away because of the lockdown. They didn't know she had already ended the relationship.

The landlady, who had become a close friend, visited Nandini daily. They were around the same age and often shared conversations. As the days went on, her friend grew concerned and urged Nandini to go stay with her husband, worrying about how long this "house arrest" might last. Nandini couldn't bring herself to reveal that she and Aakash were no longer together.

The pandemic taught everyone hard lessons—especially how to live a simpler life without the luxuries we'd once relied on.

Nandini called Aakash, and after just two rings, he picked up. "Hello, Aakash. How are you? I hope everything is fine at home."

"Hi. Yes, all is well. Are you still in Delhi, or did you manage to go home?" Aakash asked.

"No, how could I? There are no transports available," Nandini replied.

"Hope everything's fine with your family," Aakash inquired.

"Yes, all good. I didn't want to bother you, but I'm in a bit of a situation. My landlady has started asking about you. She noticed you haven't visited in a while, and with the pandemic, she's panicking. She keeps insisting I move to your place, which obviously isn't possible," Nandini explained.

"Didn't you tell her you dumped me?" Aakash responded, his tone cold and arrogant.

"How could I say that to her? I could only ask for your help. If you don't want to come, it's okay," Nandini said calmly, hiding her frustration.

"I can come, but since you broke up with me, I have a girlfriend now. If you're okay with that, I'll visit," Aakash replied shamelessly.

Nandini was taken aback. How could someone move on so quickly after being in a relationship for 10-12 years? She wondered but didn't let her thoughts show.

Actually, the fact is It's really easy for an unfaithful partner to walk away because they already have their next option lined up. It's harder for the loyal partner to walk away because they weren't looking for happiness elsewhere.

"Yeah, you can come. It's your life and your decision. Who am I to judge?" Nandini responded with composure.

She knew Aakash would come. Being in the media, he wasn't restricted by the same lockdown rules, and he could travel without much hassle.

Aakash returned to Nandini's place as if nothing had changed. He brought drinks, snacks, ice cubes—just like old times. It didn't feel like six months had passed since their last meeting.

Nandini was prepared for his visit, knowing she had little choice. He arrived in the evening, casually entering, placing the bottles in the fridge, and sanitising his hands before sitting in the corner.

Nandini, in an attempt to refresh her mood, had put on a little makeup after being confined to her home for months. But despite the effort, an awkward silence filled the room. Neither of them spoke. Aakash grabbed the TV remote and began flipping through the news, as if it were any ordinary day. Fifteen minutes passed, and Aakash, familiar with everything in Nandini's home, got up, took the bottles from the fridge, and poured drinks for both of them.

He handed her a glass without saying a word. Nandini, overwhelmed by the familiarity of it all, watched him in silence. She took small sips, observing Aakash move around the space they once shared.

They finished the first round, and Aakash stood up to prepare a second.

Suddenly, Nandini's emotions, bottled up for so long, overwhelmed her. She felt a surge of tears welling up. Without thinking, she moved closer to Aakash and hugged him tightly, her body trembling. "How could you not contact me for all these months?" she asked, her voice cracking.

In that moment, she forgot everything else—all the pain, all the distance. All she wanted was to feel the connection they once had, to hold onto what had slipped away.

Aakash, caught off guard, held her close. He kissed her, almost desperately, as if trying to make sense of the sudden emotional flood. They stumbled toward the bedroom, lost in the moment, and Aakash whispered, "Why did you leave, Nandini? Why did you let me go? How could you do this to me?"

Wrapped in each other's arms, they gave in to the feelings they had been trying to bury for so long. Nandini's tears flowed freely as they melted into each other, letting the past and present blur together, if only for that brief, fragile moment.

After an hour, Aakash got up from the bed, finished his drink, and asked Nandini to shut the door. He told her that he would come again. Nandini fell asleep soon after he left her apartment.

Akash began visiting every week again, but things were different now. He would only stay for a few hours—just enough time to drink, eat, have sex, and leave. It was always about four hours. Nandini didn't complain, didn't argue, and simply accepted this routine.

One day, after six months of this pattern, during an intimate moment, Nandini finally asked Aakash if he was still seeing the other woman. He denied it, saying he had stopped seeing her since the lockdown ended and for other reasons as well. Though Nandini had her doubts, she didn't feel the need to argue.

Their relationship began to heal again, slowly but surely. In the meantime, Aakash got a new job at a bigger media company. When Nandini's neighbour heard the good news, they asked her to throw a party to celebrate. Nandini agreed, feeling hopeful that this might be a fresh start for both of them.

Chapter IX

Two years passed, and life slowly returned to normal. Offices reopened, and everything seemed to be falling back into place. But then, Nandini faced a major change in her life. She had to make the difficult decision to resign from her job and move back to her hometown.

Her father had passed away a few years earlier, her daughter had completed her studies and secured a job, and her mother's health was declining. Nandini knew it was time to be closer to her family. Though Aakash tried to convince her to stay, suggesting she bring her mother to live with her instead, Nandini knew her mother would never agree to leave. She promised Aakash that she would visit him whenever possible and that the distance wouldn't change their bond. Deep down, she hoped that this separation might even make Aakash realise her value when he could no longer see her so easily.

Nandini moved back home, and Aakash helped arrange everything she needed. He never missed a day without calling her. But soon, his own life took a turn when his mother fell seriously ill. With both his office and caring for his mother, Aakash found it hard to visit Nandini, though they stayed in touch.

Even though Nandini resigned from her job, her company didn't accept her resignation. Since she had worked remotely during the COVID lockdown, they offered her the option to continue working from her hometown. Then, unexpectedly, she got a chance to visit Delhi for work. Overjoyed, Nandini looked forward to reuniting with Aakash, as well as her old friends and colleagues.

Aakash stayed connected with Nandini in every possible way, always showing deep concern whenever she seemed distant. Every night after work, he made sure to call her, and they would talk for hours. On every special occasion, Aakash sent her thoughtful gifts, and he never missed a chance to wish her well. His care extended not just to Nandini but also to her family, showing his genuine concern. Though Aakash wasn't the most expressive person, his actions made Nandini feel that his love was real. Sometimes, distance reveals the true strength of a relationship.

A year later, she finally arrived in Delhi. She had already told Aakash, and he came to pick her up from the airport before dropping her off at her office. Nandini's current office is in Gurgaon now. In the meantime, Aakash's family had bought a new, larger house, and Aakash had also bought a new car. Nandini, having witnessed his journey from the very beginning, insisted on visiting his new home, meeting his family, and especially checking on his ailing mother. It felt like the right thing to do as an old friend, and Aakash agreed.

Nandini visited Aakash's new house for the first time, and there was another good news awaiting her. Although Aakash wasn't married, his brother had recently tied the knot, and the family had been blessed with twins. Nandini, who always adored children, was overjoyed when Aakash shared the news of the twins' birth. Excited to meet the family, she brought gifts for everyone, as it was her first time meeting them.

Aakash picked Nandini up from her hotel and took her to his home to meet the family. Although it was their first time meeting in person, Nandini had known about them for years through her long-standing relationship with Aakash. She felt an instant connection, like a family friend. Aakash even suggested she stay at their new house instead of the hotel, but Nandini declined, feeling it wasn't appropriate since the rest of the family didn't know her well yet.

To her surprise, Nandini received a warm and gracious welcome. Aakash's mother, his brother, sister-in-law, and the little twins embraced her with open arms, offering her a grand reception. Nandini couldn't help but wonder why she hadn't met them earlier when she lived in Delhi. After a wonderful visit, Aakash dropped her back at the hotel. His sister-in-law even invited Nandini to meet again during her trip, and Nandini happily accepted the invitation.

Just three days after Nandini's visit to Aakash's place, his sister-in-law Shilpa arranged another meeting, this time inviting Nandini to join them for dinner. To Nandini's surprise, they had invited her alone, without Aakash knowing anything about it. This unexpected invitation made Nandini uneasy, as she had a feeling there was more to it than just a casual dinner.

Aakash's younger brother Nikhil and his lovely wife Shilpa came to Nandini's hotel to pick her up, and they took her to a five-star hotel for dinner. Nandini was again taken aback, as she couldn't quite understand why they were showing her such warmth and attention. Before heading out, she had asked Aakash how she should respond if they asked about her relationship with him. Aakash reassured her, telling her she could be honest and didn't need to worry about hiding anything.

This eased Nandini's nerves a little, as she despised lying. She believed that telling one lie only led to a web of more lies, something she never wanted to get tangled in. With Aakash's blessing to speak the truth, she felt slightly more comfortable heading into the dinner, though still unsure of what lay ahead.

Nandini's instincts were spot on – they had caught on to her relationship with Aakash. During the dinner, Nikhil and Shilpa wanted to know everything about her and Aakash. Nikhil was shocked to learn that Nandini and Aakash had been dating for fourteen long years, and he couldn't understand why his brother had kept it a secret from the rest of the family.

Shilpa, Aakash's sister-in-law, took things a step further and requested Nandini to consider marrying Aakash. She expressed her concern, especially since Nandini and Aakash had been together for so long, and with Aakash's mother's declining health, Shilpa wanted to arrange the marriage as soon as possible.

Nandini, however, was caught off guard and felt unable to make any decision without Aakash knowing what was happening. She urged them to talk to Aakash directly about the proposal, reminding them that marriage is a serious matter, especially when it's a second marriage. Deep down, Nandini knew Aakash had never been interested in marriage, even from the beginning of their relationship.

Feeling the pressure, Nandini gently declined their proposal, saying that at her age, she couldn't consider remarriage. But Shilpa continued to plead with her to think it over again. After the conversation, they dropped Nandini back at her hotel and asked if they could meet her again during her trip.

Chapter X

Nandini picked up the phone and called Aakash, her voice steady but with a hint of concern. She needed to tell him what had happened at the restaurant the other night. Aakash, caught off guard, listened as Nandini explained how his brother and sister-in-law had brought up the idea of marriage—between her and Aakash—without ever discussing it with him. He was shocked and angry.

"How could my family do this without even asking me?" Aakash snapped, his frustration evident.

Nandini understood his reaction well. "I already told them no," she reassured him softly. "But they asked me to reconsider. They'll be coming again to talk."

She could sense Aakash's hesitation. He wasn't the type to rush into marriage, and if he had wanted this, he would have acted long ago. Nandini knew deep down that she would struggle to fit into his family's life. Having lived on her own for years, the thought of adjusting to a North Indian joint family—especially with all the cultural and lifestyle differences—felt overwhelming.

Two days later, Shilpa, Aakash's sister-in-law, called again. She was eager to meet Nandini, insisting that the family had started talking about the marriage among themselves—without Aakash's involvement. Nandini was stunned. "They haven't even asked him?" she questioned.

Shilpa ignored her concerns and pushed her to think it over, assuring her they'd take care of everything. Nandini agreed to meet Shilpa again, curious but also a little hesitant.

That evening, Shilpa came alone to pick her up from her hotel. They spent hours talking, and Nandini found Shilpa to be a modern, open-minded woman. There was mutual respect between them, and Shilpa opened up about Aakash's distant behaviour. "He never participates in family matters," Shilpa complained. "We're all frustrated with him. But maybe if he marries you, things will change."

Nandini listened, understanding Shilpa's heartfelt plea. But her mind was elsewhere. Could she really see herself in this family? She explained her concerns to Shilpa, especially the long commute from her job in Gurgaon to Aakash's home. "I wouldn't be able to live with your family full time. I could only come on weekends," Nandini said frankly.

To her surprise, Shilpa agreed. She even invited Nandini over for lunch that Sunday, eager to finalise the marriage soon.

After returning to her hotel, Nandini called Aakash and shared the details of the conversation. He listened, but his tone was indifferent.

That Sunday, Nandini made up her mind. After speaking with her family and friends, she realised she couldn't marry Aakash. Her past experiences with him, especially the bitterness in Delhi, had left scars. Aakash was a good friend, but he wasn't the life partner she needed. Unable to face Shilpa directly, Nandini recorded a voice message, explaining her reasons for declining the proposal.

Later that evening, Aakash showed up at her hotel, visibly angry. "How could you reject the proposal without talking to me first?" he shouted, his frustration boiling over. "They didn't even talk to me about it! Everyone's avoiding me!"

Nandini was taken aback. "Aakash, just yesterday you weren't even sure about marriage. How could I agree to something you don't want? This isn't a joke—it's a marriage!"

Aakash's expression softened but only slightly. "I can't go against my family's wishes. If they want me to marry you, I will."

Nandini shook her head gently. "I'm not marrying a family, Aakash. I'm marrying a man. And if we were to get married, I wouldn't be able to live with your family full time. My job is too far."

"You can't live alone!" Aakash protested. "Another woman in our family manages both work and home. Why can't you?"

Nandini felt a wave of confusion. What did Aakash really want? Did he even want this marriage, or was he just trying to please his family?

Taking a deep breath, she finally asked, "Aakash, what about the girlfriend you told me about? Are you still in touch with her?"

He quickly shook his head. "That's in the past. There's nothing now. I barely have time for myself, let alone someone else. Between work, my plant business, and helping my mother, I'm exhausted."

Aakash seemed sincere, but his words did little to calm Nandini's doubts.

"They want this to happen fast, but I need more time," Aakash admitted. "Give me another two years."

Nandini smiled sadly. "Two years? Who knows what tomorrow will bring, Aakash?"

In her heart, Nandini understood what was really happening. Aakash was stalling, trying to buy time. But she knew that no matter how much time passed, this marriage wasn't meant to be.

Chapter XI

Nandini returned to her hometown with a heart full of mixed emotions. She carried gifts from Aakash's family, along with precious memories of their warm gestures. Despite Aakash never showing much interest in introducing Nandini to his family, she discovered how deeply they cared for one another. Their strong bond and genuine thoughtfulness towards each other touched Nandini's soul in ways she hadn't expected, having lived alone for so many years.

Though she initially thought Aakash, and his family might not bring up the marriage again, she was pleasantly surprised when everyone continued to stay in touch with her after she returned from Gurgaon. Even Aakash began to talk more about what their future together might look like. Gradually, Nandini started to believe that maybe this marriage could actually happen one day.

One thing that tugged at Nandini's heart was the twin children in Aakash's family. Having been separated from her own daughter during her childhood, she had missed those precious moments of watching her grow. Motherhood, to her, was the most beautiful phase of a woman's life. Nandini began to wonder if perhaps, through these twins, she could relive those moments she had lost.

As more time passed, the winter lingered unusually long. Aakash, always mindful of Nandini's early bedtime, called her each night by 9:30 p.m. On January 26th, however, he called earlier than usual, around 7 p.m. Nandini missed the call, busy with household chores, and planned to return it once she was free.

At 8:30 p.m., her phone rang again, this time from an unknown number. Normally, she wouldn't have answered—most unknown numbers were spam. But destiny had other plans. A woman's voice greeted Nandini, asking for her name and confirming her profession. Puzzled but polite, Nandini answered the questions.

Ten minutes later, the same woman called back, introducing herself as Aakash's girlfriend. She claimed they had been in a relationship for many years. Shock washed over Nandini, leaving her speechless. How could this be true? Who was this woman? Desperate for answers, Nandini tried to call Aakash, but his line was busy. Feeling helpless, she called Shilpa, Aakash's sister-in-law, to verify the claim.

Shilpa was equally stunned by the story. She tried to reassure Nandini that it could be a misunderstanding, urging her to talk to Aakash directly.

A few minutes later, Aakash finally called back, apologising and admitting that the woman's claims were true. He explained that there was an emergency—his mother had fallen ill and was being rushed to the hospital. Begging Nandini for understanding, he asked her not to punish his mother for his mistakes.

Nandini couldn't process what was happening. How could the man she had trusted for 15 years betray her so deeply? The ground beneath her feet seemed to disappear.

For two days, Nandini shut herself off from the world. She refused to take calls, couldn't sleep, and lost all appetite. The betrayal left her shattered. In her distress, she confided only in her daughter, the one person she could trust. Her daughter, who had known Aakash since childhood, was equally shocked and angered by the revelation.

Two days later, the mysterious woman called again. This time, she fully introduced herself as Bipasha. She explained that she had been involved with Aakash for over five years. Bipasha was separated from her husband and had two children. Aakash, she said, had been visiting her regularly, all while claiming to have been in a relationship with another woman from his past. Bipasha revealed how Aakash had deceived them both, playing with their emotions for years.

Nandini couldn't fathom how Aakash could plan a marriage with her while being involved with someone else. The betrayal felt like a deep wound, and she no longer knew who she was in the eyes of those around her. Her social dignity, her self-respect, everything she had carefully built over the years, felt ruined in a matter of hours.

Consumed by anger and heartbreak, Nandini woke up the next morning, determined to take control of the situation. She gathered every gift Aakash had ever given her in their 15 years together. She made a list of each item, wrote a letter, and sent everything back to Aakash's home. She also sent a copy of the letter and list to Bipasha as a witness, ensuring that the chapter with Aakash was closed for good.

Nandini realised she was stronger than she ever imagined. No one would play with her heart again.

Chapter XII

Nandini had hoped that Aakash might apologise and ask to rebuild their relationship, but things turned out quite differently.

After Nandini spoke with Shilpa and shared everything she learned from Bipasha, Aakash felt humiliated. His pride was hurt, especially in the eyes of his family. His male ego couldn't bear the thought that Nandini had taken such bold steps. He returned all the gifts she had sent and felt betrayed by her actions.

Two days later, Aakash called Nandini, but instead of making amends, he lashed out at her. He yelled, "How dare you talk to everyone in my family about this?" His anger knew no bounds. He made it clear that he had chosen Bipasha over Nandini and that he would never marry her. Their conversation turned into a shouting match, leaving Nandini stunned at his harsh, abusive behaviour. It felt as if *"the thief was scolding the guard,"* turning the tables as if Nandini was at fault.

Nandini had never been humiliated like this before. The weight of Aakash's words crushed her self-respect. She realised she could no longer endure this emotional abuse and made a firm decision.

*** *** *** ****

Nandini couldn't understand if it was day or night. Everything felt like a blur. Pain coursed through her body as she faintly heard someone calling her name, "Nandini... Nandini... how are you feeling now?" She tried to move but couldn't. Slowly, she opened her eyes and saw a figure, likely a doctor, standing over her.

After 5-6 days in the hospital, the memories came flooding back. She had attempted suicide. On the night of February 9th, after a heated argument with Aakash, she swallowed twenty sleeping pills, wanting to end the pain. But even death refused her. Now, Nandini was left in a deep depression, her spirit broken. She stopped talking to everyone, sinking further into anxiety. Despite counselling and medical treatment, Nandini remained unresponsive, lost in her grief.

The doctor suggested a change of scenery, maybe a trip, to help lift her spirits. But Nandini resisted, not wanting to go anywhere. Her mother was heartbroken, but it was Nandini's daughter, Priyanka, who took responsibility with patience and love. Priyanka, who now worked for a multinational company, knew the struggles her mother had faced. She became Nandini's constant support, caring for her day and night, determined to bring back her mother's happiness.

Priyanka, understanding her mother's need for human connection, made a new social media profile for Nandini. She carefully selected thoughtful, positive people to add to her mother's circle, hoping to bring a smile back to her face. It was through this effort that they connected with Adarsh.

Two months later, Priyanka arranged a meeting between her mother and Adarsh. She was confident her mother would like him. Priyanka and Adarsh had been chatting regularly, and she had told him everything about Nandini's struggles. Adarsh, a psychology doctorate and motivational corporate leader, was kind and empathetic. Priyanka knew he understood human emotions well and believed he could be the perfect person to help her mother heal.

Priyanka had already encouraged her mother to speak with Adarsh twice over the phone. She liked him and was certain that Adarsh could be the light Nandini needed to move forward in her life.

Two more months passed, and Adarsh proposed to Nandini. She accepted, knowing that the past was behind her, and everyone deserves a loving, caring partner to share life's journey. Nandini recognised that Adarsh was a kind-hearted, transparent person—someone who would never hurt her. She agreed to the marriage, and Priyanka was thrilled with her mother's decision. Slowly, Nandini returned to her old self, smiling again and resuming her work. In June, Nandini and Adarsh got married.

However, there were still moments when something from the past haunted Nandini. She shared these feelings with her doctor, understanding that she was still healing. Yet, with Adarsh by her side, the healing process felt faster. Nandini knew that Adarsh loved her even more deeply than she could express, and he accepted her with all her scars, knowing that time would eventually heal everything.

After two months of marriage, Nandini decided to take a trip. She wanted to confront Aakash one last time to find closure. She believed it was necessary to stand before him and finally close that chapter of her life. She called him twice during her trip, but Aakash showed no interest in meeting her. Nandini eventually gave up, realising that the pain would remain for both of them, unresolved.

Everything between them had ended over the phone without a proper goodbye. Each time Aakash had brought up the same topic: how Nandini had left him with just a message, never reaching out to him for six months. It was as if he had taken revenge on her for what had happened before the pandemic, and Bipasha had only made things worse, driving the final wedge.

Now, Nandini had one day left before she was to leave. She was struggling to sleep, knowing that without enough rest, it would be difficult for her to function at work. The phone rang at 2 a.m. It was Aakash.

For the first time in six months, they spoke again.

"Did you really get married? Bipasha showed me a picture you sent her two months ago. Who's that guy? Where did you meet him? What's his name?" Aakash's voice was rushed, unlike his usual calm self.

Nandini smiled softly to herself. "Does it really matter, Aakash? You called me in the middle of the night just to ask this? Are you serious?" she replied gently.

"You don't get it! I was with someone else, but that doesn't make me a criminal. Why are you treating me like one?" Aakash snapped.

Nandini sighed. "Aakash, I know you were just trying to get back at me. It's fine. I'm not here to argue with you at midnight."

"No! You have to listen to me!" Aakash's voice broke as he suddenly began crying. "Did you know my mom passed away? And then two of my other relatives... I've been dealing with it all alone."

"You never understood my pain, Nandini. You left me too, remember? You dumped me three years ago with just a note," he cried.

Nandini's voice rose in frustration. "How many times do I have to tell you? I never left you! I just wanted to see what you'd do if I stepped away. But you never came for me, Aakash. Never called. Why do you always blame me?"

"Because you did this, Nandini!" Aakash shouted back. "You knew I couldn't handle rejection. I thought maybe you found someone new because I didn't give you enough time. And you told me to act maturely, so I didn't reach out then."

"Where did you get married, Nandini? Does your family know, or did you just do it on your own?" Aakash asked again, desperate.

Nandini was stunned by his questions. "Why would I hide anything, Aakash? It's a marriage, not a game, unlike the one you played with me."

"Yes, I'm the bad guy," Aakash said bitterly. "I played with your emotions. I don't have a heart. Is he good to you? Are you happy with him?"

Nandini paused, unsure of how to respond. "Aakash, it's over. You made your choices, and I made mine. These words won't change anything now. Please stop crying and get some sleep. I have to be at the office by 9 a.m., and I need rest."

"If it's really over, why did you ask to meet me? Why, Nandini? You know I can't express myself," Aakash pleaded, his voice still shaking.

"I asked you to meet so we could have closure. Every relationship needs that, or else it'll haunt us forever," Nandini explained softly.

"I can't come alone. Bipasha's your friend now, right? Call her. I'll come with her. You know I can't say anything. I'll just sit there. Where are you staying?" Aakash asked.

Nandini's voice hardened. "If you can't come alone, then don't come at all, Aakash. And for the record, Bipasha is not my friend. She's your girlfriend. I know you can't face me, but when you find the courage, we can meet in a public place—not at my hotel."

With that, Nandini ended the call, knowing the pain would linger for both of them. But it was time to move on. Their paths had diverged, and though the wounds would take time to heal, she had chosen her future—a future without Aakash.

Some stories are simply meant to remain incomplete, their beauty lying in the unfinished chapters where hearts still whisper, and memories linger like a fading melody. In those untold moments, where the words remain unsaid and the paths never fully cross, there is a quiet elegance. The silence between the lines speaks volumes, holding the fragments of emotions that time refuses to erase. It's in those unfinished stories that the soul finds solace, knowing that sometimes, not all endings need to be written to be felt.

The End

The Destiny

Chapter I

"Have you felt it before?"

"No, I haven't," I said.

"Trust me, we are the mirror reflection of each other."

"How can that be possible?"

"What is that, a mirror reflection? What does it do? How is it made? Who makes them?"

"Just take a deep breath. It may take some time, but soon you'll start feeling it too. Trust me," he said.

Oops... Sorry, I just forgot to introduce him. "Hi, this side it's Mehul. Mehul from Mumbai. Your name is very unique, though it's also quite common. Chini, right? Can I call you Chinu?" he said.

"Yeah, hi! Nice to meet you here. Yes, you can call me Chinu. And welcome to my page. By the way, your name is very unique too. 'Mehul' sounds so nice. I've never heard this name before. What does it mean?"

"The rain drops," he said.

"Wow, beautiful! Do you know I love the rain? In my childhood, during the rainy season, I used to drench myself in the rain on the way back from school with one of my friends."

"Childhood memories are so precious," I told him.

"Yes, dear, you're right. Childhood memories are always precious. They transport us to another world. The older we grow, the more those memories mesmerise us," he said.

"You're so interesting to talk to! I feel so comfortable speaking with you! It's like I've known you for so many days!"

"If I said I've known you even from our past life..." he said.

"Sorry, what do you mean? Mehul, if you came here to flirt with me, then this isn't the right place for you."

"I'm sorry if you feel that way, but it wasn't my intention. You've misunderstood me. I've just told you the same thing you told me, and yes, I feel the same way about you. I'm not lying or flirting. Why would I? We're not at that age, and no one has time for such cheap things. Time is precious, right? We all come from an educated background."

"Hey, then what do you want? Why are you talking like this? Listen, I'm already engaged. It's better to let you know clearly about my status. I don't want any misunderstanding."

"Great news, dear. I'm so happy for you. Many, many congratulations. God bless you, dear," he said. "It's really great news!"

What is that? Is he mad? "Yeah, thank you so much."

"So, how long have you been dating that person?" he asked.

"Nope, we haven't started dating yet. Well, actually, yes, we've been dating online for the past few days, and we're going to meet soon." "Why do I feel like you're laughing? Listen, I'm in a serious relationship, and don't laugh."

"Dear, who said I'm laughing? Why would I? It's your life, you're mature enough, and you can make your own decisions. Who am I to judge you? Trust in God. Whatever happens, happens for the best," he said.

"True. Thank you so much for your wishes. I'm leaving now; I have lots of work. I'll catch up with you later. Bye, take care."

"Sure, it was nice talking to you. God bless you."

Chapter II

"Mehul, you've got me all confused now. What do you know about me that makes you say the guy must be lucky to have me?"

"You're very special, dear, very special. Whoever has you in their life will be a very lucky person," he said.

"तुम तो ऐसे बोल रहे हो, जैसे ना जाने तुम कबसे मुझे जानते हो!" (Mehul, you talk as if you've known me for a long time!)

"Mehul, can I tell you something? Do you know, I'm actually very scared deep inside my heart."

"Why, dear? What's making you feel like that?" he asked.

"Mehul, I've never met anyone like this before in my whole life! It's not just about meeting someone. I'm going to stay with him for three days. You see, meeting a guy for coffee is one thing, but..."

"Start dating him—that's natural. But in my case, things are moving too fast. I know that, but I can't control myself."

"If you feel that way, then talk to him. He's a sensible person; he'll definitely understand your concerns," Mehul said.

"Mehul, I can't stop myself. I have to go; I have to meet him. But I keep thinking about my past. I was in an 18-year relationship, and then I found out he had a parallel relationship with another woman for many years. So, I can't judge people by the length of a relationship anymore. There's no guarantee that time equals loyalty. I just broke up two months ago, so the wound is still fresh. It hasn't healed yet."

"Look, if you're talking about 'forever,' I have to tell you—forever is just a myth. No one and nothing is forever. But as long as you live, make the most of it. Don't dwell on your past. Pack your bags for the future and stop looking back. I'm not saying you should forget your past—no one can forget—but there will come a time when you'll learn to live with it, with your pain. In the end, we all accept reality," he said.

"Mehul, you speak so well. When you explain things to me, I feel so calm. Who are you, Mehul? How do you know me so well? I'm sorry, but I have to say it—I'm starting to feel attracted to you." "तु सुकून है मेरे लिए क्या रिश्ता है तेरे साथ मेरा, लगता है बरसों पहले तू बिछड़ गया था, अब जाकर मिला"।।। (You are my peace. What is this bond we share? It feels like we were separated years ago and have just now reunited.)

"Do you know, we're actually the same at our core? I mean, we come from the same source, the same womb. The only difference is our gender. You are my mirror reflection." **"तू अक्स है मेरा"**, he told me that. (You are my reflection.)

"How? How do you know that? How do you feel that? Mehul, don't say that. I'm so confused right now. I'm waiting for someone else. I'm about to meet him!"

"Listen, dear, please don't panic. We are here just to support each other. We are like two sides of a river. We can run parallel but can never touch. We were born to live this way," he said.

I never hear about this form! When I read those sentences, I always feel goosebumps! How can someone be connected that way?

Chapter III

—◆◆—

"Hey, how are you? How was your trip? I'm sure you guys just hit it off. You're probably having an amazing time. I'm so happy for you, dear. God bless. Now, tell me honestly, how do you feel inside? Does he match your vibes? I'm sure he does."

"तुझे पता है ना, तू काया है, तू एक पूरा समुंदर है, तुझसे मिलना एक बात है, पर तू कहीं रुक नहीं सकती, तुझे बहते जाना है, सृष्टि का नियम है।"

(You know, don't you? You are an entire ocean. Meeting you is one thing, but you can't stop—you have to keep flowing. It's the law of the universe.)

"What are you saying, Mehul? God, I'm just normal, simple—a very average woman. That's it."

"Who says that to you? Look into my eyes—just see who you are," he said.

"How can I look into your eyes? We haven't met yet. I don't even know if we'll ever meet. I'm scared of you. I feel like I'm not whole anymore. I feel divided. Everything inside me is divided!"

"Don't be silly. Why are you talking like that? Why are you feeling divided? You're just exhausted. We've been talking a lot lately, and your mind is probably occupied with all those thoughts," he said.

"Are you mad or crazy? Don't you see what's happening? I know you like me, and I like you too, but this will affect my new relationship. He's so much into me! I'm committed to him."

"Okay, fine. From tomorrow, we won't talk much, or we'll talk less. Is that okay with you? Now, smile please. Let's go have a cup of tea. Will you want to go for a long drive?", he said.

One sudden day, I just normally checked my chat history and realised that Mehul and I had exchanged 400 text messages in a day!!

Where it's just 79 now with my boyfriend!! I am so surprised! I am so addicted to that person! We hadn't even met each other!

When I shared this with Mehul, he was also very surprised and asked me to decrease the number of messages. It's like we are trying to ration our messages.

And the very next day, in the morning, within 17 minutes, we exchanged twenty messages with each other! Mehul told me he was supposed to do these twenty messages in the whole day. Imagine!

It's an experience. You hardly find a person who will give you so much attention with respect and care. He never misbehaves; he is never judgemental. It's just amazing!

And the best part between us is we never talk about our feelings; we always talk about my personal issues, music, art, culture, mythology, heritage, cinematography, poetry, general topics, and we never think or fall into a relationship, but we cherish each other's company to make a strong bond between us which is just beyond any relationship.

He never talks about his personal matters, and I never feel like asking anything. I am so used to him that for anything and everything, I need him. He is now more than a friend to me. He is my "HOME".

कुछ रिश्तों की अहमियत उनके होने में होती है, कोई नाम नहीं होता उन रिश्तों का। बस वो होते हैं, एक धागे से बंधे हुए दो लोग, बिना किसी वजह के...

(Some relationships derive their significance from simply existing. They have no name, just two people connected by an invisible thread, without any reason.)

Emotions are hard to describe. The best relationships are those which are just without any expectations from each other.

One random night, he suddenly sent me a few pictures of his family members. I thought to myself, "Why is he sending me his family's pictures out of nowhere?" But deep down, I knew the answer. Maybe he felt it was time to share more about himself. Maybe, after two months of talking, he's finally comfortable enough to open up to me. I just smiled.

In the meantime, I met my boyfriend for the second time. And the worst part? I've started talking about Mehul with him. So, basically, I'm talking about my boyfriend when I'm chatting with Mehul, and now I'm talking about Mehul when I'm with my boyfriend.

Can you please help me understand what's going on in my head? Am I crazy? Who does that?! I've accepted that this feels wrong. So, I've started distancing myself as much as possible. We're both forcing our emotions to stay in check. We've created a mental barrier, a "check post" to guard the feelings we're developing for each other.

But for me, the more I try to control it, the more addicted I become. Now, I don't even need to chat with him—I'm chatting with myself. And it feels like I'm talking to him. Am I losing my mind?

Can someone believe this? I've started fantasising about him. I can feel him. When I close my eyes, I can feel his touch—all over. But we hardly talk anymore.

Chapter IV

Suddenly, we made plans to meet. It's set for June, right after the monsoon begins. I'm going to meet my boyfriend, and we've invited Mehul to join us.

I feel like I need to explain my true feelings for Mehul in front of my boyfriend because I don't see any other option. I need both of them in my life.

Mehul is two years older than me and is quite mature. He handles emotional imbalances so well. I've always told him to be strong because I feel like the weakest one.

He came over for lunch, and this was the first time we were meeting in person. Although we used to chat a lot, we couldn't talk much that day. He kept asking me what was wrong, why I wasn't talking, and why it felt like my body was there but not my soul.

It's true. How can I explain that my two favourite people are sitting in front of me, and I feel lost somewhere else? I was sitting opposite Mehul, and our eyes met so many times. I felt like I could only find myself in his eyes.

How does it feel for a woman to see herself reflected in the eyes of two beautiful souls who are very close to her heart? Some situations are unexpectedly overwhelming. The problem is that while our mouths can lie or hide, our eyes reveal the truth. Our eyes are the true reflection of our soul.

"तू अक्स है मेरा", Mehul told me that. Once again, I remembered that. In fact, today I truly felt that it was true.

After five hours, Mehul went back. My boyfriend and I returned to our room, and he said, "I understand that you and Mehul are very attached to each other. Mehul told me that you both have a strong platonic connection. I won't mind if you sometimes feel the need to share a physical bond as well."

I can't describe how I felt at that moment. I couldn't face his eyes or understand why he said that. How could I possibly do that? Yes, I like Mehul, and it's more than just liking, but not every relationship is meant to become physical. He might be trying to show how big his heart is.

But what about humanity and morality? How can the other person accept that? Mehul has told me many times that while he loves me, his love is expressed through true care and respect, nothing more.

He said that if we become too close, this beautiful bond would end, and he doesn't want that to happen. We can never meet in that way. I really respect him for that. I told him I would meet him at Varanasi. If there is a place where we could meet, it would be the "Ghats of Varanasi"—a divine place for two spiritual souls.

Some relationships are just reflections of light coming from the cosmic realm. They are meant for life after life, having no shape, no colour, no name, but a strong, unbroken bond.

Chapter V

I practice yoga each morning and love taking selfies during that time. I often post some of these photos on social media and share them with close friends. My bedroom has windows on the east and south sides, which I open while doing yoga. The first rays of the sun always come through the east window. Being on the 10th floor, the sunlight creates stunning reflections and bathes the room in its light, giving me a beautiful start to the day.

One day, I took a picture of myself with the sunlight falling on my face and decided to send it to Mehul. He replied quickly, "The sunshine on your face gives you a glowing aura, and the silver-grey hairs on your left forehead give you a regal look."

I had never seen myself in that way through someone else's eyes. I was spellbound by such a beautiful compliment about my appearance. It was beyond anything I had ever imagined.

I replied with a smiley emoji, "Mehul, people give so many compliments on a lady's photo, but no one sees it like you do. You're amazing!"

He replied, "तू प्यार है किसी और का, मुझे तेरी आँखों के नीचे उतरने का इजाज़त नहीं है। I can't go beneath your eyes."

I keep smiling silently. I can't resist myself from sharing that quote with my boyfriend just to make him feel secure that Mehul is a valuable jewel; he need not feel insecure about him. Mehul knows well his limits and boundaries. He respects me a lot.

"Do you understand what you mean to me?" Mehul said. "I could not let my eyes go below your face when you sent me the picture. It was a simple picture, and eventually, you posted a similar picture on Facebook too. But my affection for you is beyond physical, dear, and I won't let it affect our equation."

I asked him, "What does it mean, Mehul? Please explain it to me."

He said, "Love has so many definitions. Ours is love too, Chinu, but the world can't understand it."

"Ours is not about always being together and "एक दूसरेको पाना"... Our love is about being there for the person".

"You are a lovely soul, a free spirit, and honest. We are connected in that space. Our connection transcends 20 to 25 years; it cuts across births. We have to remain in each other's aura, not attempt to merge."

"You love your boyfriend, and that is something very beautiful. He is possessive about you, but I am not. He has a fear of losing you, but I know I will never lose you."

"पाने की चाहत,.... पाने से कही ज़ादा होते है", ("The desire to attain is often far greater than actually attaining.")

That is why the best love stories are the ones that never happened.

Meet me while I'm alive

Complete our story; strive!

Let our love story thrive!

Take it in your stride,

Come to me, fly or ride!

Meet me while I am still alive,

Let God read our story, so naive!

Incomplete story, I don't like!

Make it complete, give me pride!

Meet me while I'm still alive!

I'll close my eyes and lay my head.

On your chest,

While I'm around, hug me,

Not in my afterlife!

Don't tell me our souls shall meet one day!

Don't hold our meet, don't keep it.

At bay!

I know our bodies. I don't know.

What are our souls!

I know how to touch; I don't know how to

Imagine,

Imagination is a useless fabric.

Full of holes!

Meet me while I'm still alive!

Meet me, come and give me a

High – five.

Chapter – VI

After I came back from my boyfriend's place, Mehul and I hardly had time to talk. Although we used to talk a lot, discussing almost every topic, we never crossed the line.

Mehul always said, "As a person who respects you and knows about your journey, I will never attempt to get any closer than this. You know that well."

The best part about him is that he always gives his opinion neutrally on any aspect. And when my boyfriend and I have a fight, he always steps in to help me understand why my boyfriend acted or said something. He's so comfortable to talk with.

He knows exactly which words can calm me down when I'm angry. So, basically, he is the best judge of all my immature, imperfect behaviour.

Sometimes, there are issues I can't share with my boyfriend, but I can easily share them with him, knowing he won't judge me and will offer the best possible solution for that particular incident.

I can easily express what I'm feeling and why, and he always has the answer. I can't discuss my ex-boyfriend with anyone, but I can easily talk about it with Mehul.

So, when our conversations decreased, I sometimes felt shattered. I'd go on social media, trying to make new friends, but after talking for 2-3 days, I'd get bored. I couldn't match the vibes I had with Mehul.

After a few days, when Mehul had time, we started chatting like before. Suddenly, I saw a sentence appear on my phone: "You have a beauty spot on the left side of your tummy." He wrote this line.

I was spellbound, and more than that, I was surprised—how does he know that? This sudden comment made me feel embarrassed.

I stayed silent, not knowing what to say. He explained, assuming I was checking if it was really there, "No need to check further, you have it." I felt so ashamed.

He continued, "You were sitting in front of me and suddenly got up. While talking to you, for a brief moment, I saw the brownish beauty spot, and after a microsecond, I turned my head away."

Just imagine my situation—my cheeks turned red. I couldn't even read the message properly, feeling so embarrassed. Thank God it was all happening over chat and not face-to-face!

I knew I needed to reply with something, so I wrote, "How did you see that? You told me you never look below my face, so how did this happen?"

He responded, "You were wearing a saree, and when you stood up for a moment, your saree pleats shifted slightly. I was looking at your face, and suddenly, I noticed it. Within a fraction of a second, I turned my face away."

I murmured to myself, "For God's sake, Mehul, please keep your mouth shut. Why don't you understand you're embarrassing me!"

I know we've discussed almost every intimate detail of life, even how my boyfriend makes love to me, and I never thought about the fact that he, too, is a man who is quite attached to me. But still, I can't accept this from him.

I am really a crazy woman!

My thinking is he was sitting for almost 3 hours in front of me. I have a beauty spot on my eyes, on my ears. But he didn't mention that! He noticed that one which is very unexpected!

Do I like his observation?

One sudden day, in the morning, I really felt very down and missed Mehul a lot, so I wrote something for him.

<u>ख़र्च हो रही है ज़िंदगी...</u>

ख़र्च हो रही है ज़िंदगी,

थोड़ी-थोड़ी, रोज़ ख़र्च होरही है...

पिघल रही है बर्फ़, थोड़ी-थोड़ी, धीरे-धीरे, रोज़-रोज़

वो मिट्टी के मटके में जो पानी भरके रखा था...

ख़र्च हो रहा है रोज़...

क्या मिला और क्या नहीं,अब थोड़ा भूलने भी लगी हूँ,

हिसाब में पहले से कच्ची थी

अब थोड़ा और पिघलने लगी हूँ...।

ख़र्च हो रही है ज़िंदगी,

थोड़ी-थोड़ी, रोज़ रोज़...

न कोई शमा जली, न कोई परवाना...

न कोई ख़ौफ़, न कोई दिलकशी...

अब तो बस जिंदगी थोड़ी और बाक़ी बची...

गिले शिकवे अब सब मिट गए...

चाहत की ख़्वाहिश में न जाने कहाँ से कहाँ

मंज़िल तक पहुँच गए...

अब बस थोड़ी सी बची है...

एक आधा गिलास यादें, और थोड़ा सा सुकुन...

सोचा था बारिश की बूंदों से फिर एक बार भर लूंगी..

वो जो मिट्टी का मटका पड़ा है आधा खाली...

अब बस थोड़ी सी ही बची है...ये ज़िंदगी।

आधी भरी... और आधी खाली...

श्रॉफ तेरा चीनू

I hadn't received any message from him for the last 2-3 days, so I was very upset. Suddenly, I got his reply after sending my *shayari* to him.

"जो भरी हुई है उसे जिओ, अच्छे से, दिल से. Which you are anyways."

I got his real message. Which is actually beyond that. He wants that I will be with my boyfriend only.

So many things have changed in the past two or three months. My boyfriend is now so much closer to my heart, and we've built a bond that feels unbreakable. He met my family, and they all liked him a lot. I'm happy for him and for us.

Yet, at times, there's this lingering feeling of loneliness. It's like something is missing, something I can't quite put into words. I know what it is, but I can't express it to anyone. The person I used to share everything with, the one who understood me like no one else, is no longer there for me. And no one can ever take his place.

I know he's absent by choice, but that doesn't make it any easier.

Chapter VII

I love rain, and I adore swimming in it. It's my habit to swim alone in the pool in the morning, and during the monsoon, it gives me a supreme feeling.

By birth, my element is earth, which might be the reason why I feel so calm and peaceful in the water. There is an unwritten bond between earth and Water. Each raindrop signifies Mehul to me. I never miss swimming in the rain, as I feel his touch with every drop. The drops that fall on my forehead, my cheeks, my lips, my neck, my chest, my tummy, and my feet—all give me the sensation of his fingers.

It's a divine feeling. Every rainy morning, I experience the sense of bathing with my "Twin Flame."

Mehul, do you know what a "Twin Flame" is? I asked him

Let me explain it to you. A Twin Flame is a concept that describes a profound connection between two people who are believed to be "two halves of one whole." Twin Flames are also referred to as "mirror souls."

Mehul: "Wow, that sounds intriguing. What is the significance of Twin Flames?"

- Intense: Twin Flames often experience an immediate sense of recognition and intense attraction.

- Unique: This type of connection is unique and cannot be shared with anyone else on earth.

- Fated: Twin Flames are believed to be destined to reunite with one another.

- Soulful: These connections are considered spiritual or soulful.

- Similar: Twin Flames typically share a life path, pain, trauma, values, interests, and morals.

"Do you feel that ever Mehul?" I asked.

"Yes, I do," he said. "I think I feel the same for you," Mehul replied.

After many days, we finally started chatting again. Last month was my birthday, and he was supposed to join the celebration, but he didn't show up. I asked him to meet me once his crisis was over, and he agreed. However, when he found out that I was going to meet my boyfriend again, he said it was a good idea and that he would meet me there instead of coming to my city.

I understood—he doesn't want to meet me alone. I smiled, knowing he's not comfortable with it. But I couldn't help wondering, what is it that he's trying to avoid? Why doesn't he want to meet me alone?

Some bonds are meant to last a lifetime. They don't require constant communication or regular meetings. They are simply meant to be.

We never complain to each other about not calling or not meeting. We both know that a part of our soul is already reserved for each other. No matter what happens, I know that if I'm ever in trouble, he'll be there for me, and the same goes for him.

वो कहते हैं ना, मांगने से तो भगवान भी मिल जाते हैं, पर हमने ज़रूरत नहीं समझी, मांगना मुनासिब नहीं था... कुछ रिश्तों की बुनियाद अंदर से इतनी मज़बूत होती है कि बाहर की कोई भी ताकत उसको मिटा नहीं सकती।

("They say that even God can be attained through asking, but I didn't feel the need to ask, as it didn't seem appropriate... Some relationships are so deeply rooted from within that no external force can destroy them.")

If you have one person like this in your life, you are truly the luckiest person in the world. It may take years for this person to come into your life, but when they do, you realise the timing was always meant to be. It happens because God intended it. For me, Mehul is that messenger from God, a divine soul who understands the value of a relationship.

There are times when I stand in front of the mirror and I find him there, just like he said, "You are my mirror reflection..." Now, I truly feel it, Mehul. You told me from the very first day that I would understand it someday.

God bless you, dear.

Chapter VIII

———◆◆———

Sensitive people should be treasured. They love deeply and think deeply about life. They are loyal, honest, and true. The simple things sometimes mean the most to them. They don't need to change or harden. Their purity makes them who they are.

Do you remember once you told me, "You are the beautiful painting that I always wanted to paint… You are the tune that I always wanted to hum… You are the energy that I cease to exist in, and it just goes into the abyss."

I just don't want to lose you ever…"

I just smiled as I went through it.

"तेरे साथ सन १६०० - १७०० में, लोगों का इश्क़ होता था, वो है, उनकी एक बार आवाज़ सुन ली, फिर सारी जिंदगी उसी आवाज़ की यादों में जिंदगी निकल जाती।

He told me that once. तुम एक आज़ाद रूह हो। तुम्हे कोई रोक नहीं सकता, बस तुम्हारी रूह से थोड़ी आज़ादी सीख सकते हैं"

("In the years 1600-1700, people used to fall in love in such a way that once they heard someone's voice, they would spend their entire life just remembering that voice. He told me that once.

'You are a free soul. No one can stop you, they can only learn a little freedom from your soul...')

"I know you are nowhere; you may not even exist there, but still, I am so attached to your thoughts."

If I go to a mountain, I want to shout your name there… I want to hear your name… how it will echo, from one mountain to another, and come back to me… Mehul… Mehul… Mehul…"

Once you taught me the meaning of "रायगाणी", means wastage.

"तुज़को रायगाणी का रत्ती भर का भी अंदाज़ा नहीं,

तुज़को याद है वो दिन जो कैंपस के पकडानडीओ में चलते हुए काट गया था, उसमे एक प्यार तेरे था और एक प्यार मेरा…"

Poet Sohaib Mugheera Siddiqi

("You have no idea, not even a bit, about the wastage. Do you remember that day we spent walking along the narrow paths of the campus? On that day, there was your love, … and there was my love... too")

The End